FOR MIRIAM

HOW TO BEAT THE I.R.S. AT ITS OWN GAME
Strategies to Avoid—and Fight—an Audit

SECOND EDITION

HOW TO BEAT THE I.R.S. AT ITS OWN GAME
Strategies to Avoid—and Fight—an Audit

SECOND EDITION

A M I R   D.   A C Z E L ,   P H. D.

FOUR WALLS EIGHT WINDOWS, NEW YORK

Published in the United States by:
Four Walls Eight Windows
39 West 14th Street, room 503
New York, N.Y., 10011

First printing December 1995.

Library of Congress Cataloging-in-Publication Data:
Aczel, Amir D.
[2nd ed., rev.]
How to Beat the I.R.S. at Its Own Game: Strategies to Avoid—and Fight—an Audit/by Amir D. Aczel.
  p.   cm.
Includes bibliographical references.
ISBN: 1-56858-048-7
1. Tax auditing—United States—Popular works. I. Title.
KF6314.Z9A29   1995
343.7304—dc20   94-44180
    [347.3034]   CIP

10 9 8 7 6 5 4 3 2 1

Printed in the United States

PREFACE TO THE REVISED EDITION

When this book first appeared last year, it received much attention in the media and from tax practitioners and the general public. Soon after the book's arrival at bookstores, CNN ran a story (nationwide and internationally) featuring the main findings in the book. Surprisingly, the Commissioner of the IRS agreed to be interviewed. Responding directly to questions about my book, IRS Commissioner Margaret Milner Richardson was candid in admitting that ratios of expenses to income of the kinds described here do indeed cause audits. The Commissioner further agreed that the best remedy for audits triggered by high deduction ratios is the one I am recommending in this book.[1]

While the book was recognized to contain a wealth of unique, important information that has already helped taxpayers escape the IRS audit trap, the year that passed witnessed a worsening of the audit situation for all taxpayers. The reasons involve politics. Early in 1995, Commissioner Milner Richardson announced that the IRS's audit rate will more than double from one percent to 2.21 percent of all taxpayers annually. And, if you are reading this book, you are probably not the kind of taxpayer who files the simplest of tax forms: you file sched-

---

[1]CNN, "Your Money," January 7, 1995.

ules and claim deductions that significantly raise your audit probability. In fact, with a sufficiently complicated return, your audit probability could easily top ten percent per year or more. This book will help you reduce that audit probability while at the same time letting you take advantage of the tax law so you can keep as much of your earnings as possible. This revised edition contains expanded discussions of important tax topics and more detailed and specific audit-prevention rules. New tax-related developments (there were many in 1995) have been incorporated in the book. More tax-return data were gathered in the meantime, so the numerical ratios given as guidelines for avoiding audits are more precise.

As with the first edition of this book, the effort would not have been so successful without the active help of countless tax practitioners nationwide. Indeed, the book's greatest friends have been tax professionals: CPA's, attorneys, enrolled agents, tax preparers, many of whom have written and called me with their support and thanks for writing this book. In the words of one tax professional: "Finally, a book we have all been waiting for to help us even the score with the IRS." I am grateful to all of you for your genuine interest in this project and your eagerness to help by sharing your knowledge and tax data. Again I thank my publisher, John Oakes, for his continuing encouragement and support, and many thanks to the dedicated staff at Four Walls Eight Windows: Kathryn Belden, JillEllyn Riley, and Moyra Davey.

INTRODUCTION

On an unusually sunny, almost warm, February afternoon in Boston in 1991, I came home early from work. I was eager to run upstairs and hug our little baby, Miriam, not yet a year old. But before doing so, I stopped for a moment to open our mailbox. And there it was—the letter from the IRS. That letter was to change my life. For the next two years, my wife, Debra, and I had no peace. And Miriam had to learn to walk among high piles of receipts and forms strewn all over our apartment floor, her parents spending hours sifting through the piles for a receipt or document the insatiable auditor decided he wanted to see that particular week of the many weeks of the audit. Agent L.G. did not believe in courtesy or patience or human decency. He routinely demanded that we report at his office at 8 AM, knowing full well that our baby sitter only came at 9. He would repeatedly call us at home, waking us up at 5 AM on the day of our appointment to tell us that he was ill and demand to reschedule. I know now that many of his practices were even against the IRS' own regulations for its auditors. For the longest time, we had no idea why we were chosen for the audit. "Why us?" was a question we asked ourselves almost every day.

Trying to answer this question was what finally helped bring about the end of our audit, and—more importantly—led to the research that produced this book. The audit was getting worse, and L.G. was demanding more and more information, more cancelled checks, receipts, letters from employers, documents, more time.... In trying desperately to understand exactly what it was the IRS was after in an audit, I turned to the one thing I know best: statistics. Thinking about this problem in an objective and non-personal way, I began to realize that the reason for almost every audit by the IRS had to be statistics. Since this was my area, and since I believed that I was better at it than the many statisticians employed by the IRS, I knew that I could beat them. My ensuing research on the IRS confirmed that I was right, and that I had even correctly identified the exact technique used by the agency in determining who should be audited: discriminant analysis. The statistics textbook I had written a few years earlier included almost an entire chapter on this important technique. Soon it further occurred to me that I could actually use the IRS' own technique of discriminant analysis to counter its use by IRS employees. The scheme was easy; all I needed now was a few hundred tax returns.

I began to ask around. I found that I wasn't alone, and that many in my category—professionals, independent contractors, small business owners, anyone who doesn't file the simplest tax form—get audited. And I discovered that audit victims (as well as other taxpayers) will sometimes agree to share their information with you if you can offer them a scientific way to avoid the torment in the future. Within a few months, I had a small data set of 32 individual tax returns, eighteen of which had been audited. I learned a lot from this initial group of returns, since in analyzing them I was using the same technique used by the perpetrators of the audits.

As my queries expanded, I made contact with a considerable number of tax professionals nationwide, 28 of whom volunteered to send me copies of tax returns of audited and unaudited clients (about half from each group) on the condition that these be confidential— with no names, social security numbers, or any other identifying information. Within eighteen months of starting this research project, I had amassed an impressive sample of 1,289 tax returns: 631 of which had been audited and the rest (the control group) not. Now I was finally on my way. After using my own discriminant analysis to separate the audits from the non-audits in my sample, I went on to devise a more powerful methodology. I needed to estimate with great accuracy exactly what it was that caused a tax return to be audited. Eventually, an artificial-intelligence algorithm which I programmed on a Cray-2 supercomputer gave me the perfect results I needed.

As I learned more, I became smarter about our own continuing audit. Our taxes are complicated. Since I am both a professor and an author, and since my wife also works, our tax return includes both a Schedule A and a

Schedule C. From my exciting research findings, I was able to pinpoint exactly what it was that our auditor was after. Armed with this knowledge—and the sophistication gained from having looked at so many audits and talked with so many tax professionals—my wife and I were able to take control of our case. As a final result, the IRS auditors determined that they owed us money!

CHAPTER 1

WHY YOU NEED THIS BOOK

It used to be that around a million people were audited by the IRS each year. But starting in 1995, their number is doubling to almost two and a half million taxpayers, and it may rise even further as the IRS looks for more ways to increase its tax collections and to instill renewed fear in all of us. Furthermore, people in certain groups—professionals with business and other expenses, the self employed, and others—have an even higher rate of selection for an audit. Among these professionals, an audit by the IRS is not a rare event and everyone knows at least someone who's been through the ordeal.

THE REASON FOR ALMOST ALL IRS AUDITS IS STATISTICS

The IRS selects you for an audit based on purely statistical considerations, and not because it knows that you did something "wrong". If the IRS computer determines that you look—statistically—like the type of person who, in the past, has tended to yield more money for the government as a result of an audit, then you will be audited!

YOU WILL BE AUDITED IF THE IRS IS LOOKING FOR PEOPLE WITH YOUR STATISTICAL PROFILE

An IRS audit is one of the most unpleasant experiences possible, and you will want to avoid it if you can. I know. I experienced one. Even if you were extremely careful in preparing your return, chances are you will have to pay additional tax following an audit. And with these added taxes come penalties, and interest at a rate that if charged by someone else would be considered usurious. To add to your pain, the IRS keeps your interest clock ticking even while your case remains open due to their bureaucracy and through no fault of your own.

OVER 85% OF AUDITS RESULT IN ADDITIONAL TAX ASSESSMENTS

Less than fifteen percent of all audits by the IRS result in a draw or in a refund to you. The rest—over 85%—result in additional tax assessments. And the average amount of additional tax assessed is much larger than the average refund. The total amount of money the government gains from IRS audits each year is in the billions while the total amount refunded due to audits is only in the millions.[2] Even if you end up among the lucky few who do get a refund, the amount will not begin to compensate you for the aggravation of having had an IRS agent intimidate you, scrutinize every detail of your financial life, and invade your privacy.

Surprisingly, very little has been written on how to avoid an IRS audit. The main reason for this is that the government guards the secret statistical formula—the equation the computer uses in determining whom to select for an audit—more closely than it guards military

---

[2] On April 14, 1995, IRS Commissioner Milner Richardson responded on the air to an interview with the author on the CBS Evening News. In justifying IRS audit policy, the Commissioner said that IRS audits bring in "twenty-three billion dollars a year, over three times our budget, and clearly a good deal for the government." When correspondent Ray Brady asked her if she thought this meant the IRS would keep its job, she quipped "I think we'll be around for some time to come."

secrets. It is believed that only a handful of people within the giant IRS bureaucracy know the actual formula that determines audits.

The IRS gains tremendously from distrusting you and conducting these audits. Almost every year, the IRS Commissioner goes to Congress to ask for additional millions of dollars to pay for increased audits, promising in return billions in additional tax collection. Where does the money come from? The IRS tells us that only five percent of taxpayers cheat on their returns. And yet the majority of audits produce extra tax revenues! Much of the money is obtained from you not because you cheated on your taxes and were caught, but rather because the burden of proof for every single item on your tax return lies squarely on you.

In the audit, IRS agents aggressively try to disallow whatever they can, so that anything you can't prove to their absolute satisfaction is held against you. In the eyes of your IRS case officer, you are guilty even before the audit begins. Almost all audits end with at least some disallowance of your claims. Afterwards, the IRS determines the adjustments needed in your tax bill based on the disallowances, and you pay. You will likely have to pay added tax and interest even if you appeal or go to court, and the amounts are not small. A 1988 study by the GAO (the government's General Accounting Office) found that in over half the cases, IRS agents incorrectly assessed higher taxes in their audits.[3] Table 1 on page 16

---

[3] See Schnepper, 1994, in the Bibliography.

TABLE 1: Average Audit-Resulting Payments

Colorado	$17,802	Hawaii	$3,892
Texas	$9,790	Delaware	$3,756
Alaska	$8,985	Georgia	$3,787
Maryland (&DC)	$7,532	Kentucky	$3,713
Oklahoma	$7,382	Virginia	$3,660
Arkansas	$7,318	New Mexico	$3,590
Florida	$7,289	Ohio	$3,584
Nevada	$6,570	Wisconsin	$3,382
New Jersey	$6,390	N. Carolina	$3,286
Idaho	$6,295	S. Carolina	$3,209
New York	$6,290	Washington	$3,188
Massachusetts	$5,798	Indiana	$3,180
California	$5,608	Maine	$3,069
Oregon	$5,561	Iowa	$3,049
Illinois	$5,188	Rhode Island	$2,965
Kansas	$4,901	Minnesota	$2,949
Pennsylvania	$4,670	Missouri	$2,922
Utah	$4,372	Nebraska	$2,728
Michigan	$4,315	S. Dakota	$2,629
Arizona	$4,296	Mississippi	$2,529
Tennessee	$4,199	Alabama	$2,513
Wyoming	$4,154	W. Virginia	$2,375
Louisiana	$4,140	Montana	$2,181
New Hampshire	$3,983	Vermont	$2,095
Connecticut	$3,889	N. Dakota	$1,825

(Source: Internal Revenue Service)

shows average additional tax payments resulting from audits, by state, in decreasing order.

The fact that the IRS uses a secret formula makes us all victims of statistics. The secrecy of the formula used to determine who is audited assures the IRS that one of two things will happen. Either, out of fear of an audit, you will claim on your return less than the amount to which you are entitled, thus paying more tax than necessary right when you file, or you may exceed that invisible line in the secret formula and have to pay more tax after they audit you. Either way, you lose. This is the "Catch 22" that works so well for the IRS in their game against you, the taxpayer. Is there anything you can do?

Luckily, you have me! Tax problems have been looked at by accountants and tax lawyers and they are the ones who give advice and write books on how to prepare your taxes. As you see, however, the problem of avoiding an audit is a statistical one. As a statistician and the author of a number of books and research articles on statistics, I decided to take on the IRS and to beat them at their own nasty, unfair game of statistics. The Internal Revenue Service employs scores of its own statisticians, working hard on their side to devise new ways to increase audit revenues. I wanted to find a way to make sure that you will never again have to pay more tax than you actually owe.

I conducted a careful analysis of thousands of bits of information derived from a large random sample of actual returns of people who were audited and people who were not audited. As a research statistician working on the leading edge of this science, I have continuous access to methodologies and powerful supercomputers. The statistical methods I use (which are about 15 years ahead of those currently in use by the IRS) easily cracked the secret IRS audit formula.

I was able to piece together a close picture of the actual secret code, a rule that separated statistically the returns in my sample known to have been audited by the IRS from those returns known not to have been audited. Then I tested the formula against other actual returns, and was able to predict with great accuracy (over 95%) whether or not a return was audited. My findings confirmed that I had estimated the correct formula. And furthermore, new data, which became available since the first appearance of this book last year, gave additional confirmation of the high accuracy of my findings.

In the first few chapters of the book I explain how the IRS operates. I then describe the audit process and give you some advice on what to do—and, often more importantly—what not to do in case you are audited. I discuss the secret formula and how the IRS uses it against you, and explain its reconstruction later in the book. The remaining chapters demonstrate clearly how you can benefit from my estimated formula by using simple rules to test whether or not your return is likely to be audited. I show you how to prepare and file your return in a way that will maximize the amount of money to which you are entitled while minimizing the chances of an IRS audit. No one else can give you such advice, as the national media and the tax profession quickly recognized when the book first appeared last year. After reading this book you will never again throw away money that is rightfully yours just because you were afraid of being audited. And on the other hand, you will not file a return that instantly begs the IRS computer to pick you for an audit. Of course, I need to caution you that statistics is the name of the game. So if you follow my advice you will minimize the chance of an audit. I can't give you a guarantee that you will not be audited. Returns are audited for a variety of reasons—some of which are totally out of your control or mine. But if you follow my advice, the chances of an audit will be greatly reduced and you will be much further ahead in this game. Let's even the playing field!

CHAPTER 2

A GOLIATH NAMED I.R.S.

You've been sitting in the stuffy, windowless room on the 13th floor of the Federal Building for three hours now, and the end is nowhere in sight. The gruff, middle-aged IRS agent sitting across the table from you has been writing endlessly on a yellow legal pad while referring time and again to copies of the bank statements you had to ask your bank to provide for the audit (at a cost of $144.00!—you didn't know you had to keep the original statements they send you...). Every once in a while, the agent breaks his pencil (he must be really out to get you), stands up and walks slowly over to the rusty pencil sharpener on the wall, the sound of which is beginning to give you the worst headache of your life. Eventually—weeks, perhaps months later—you end up paying lots of money as well. The agent could not balance your checkbook to his satisfaction. You had made cash deposits, mostly reimbursed job-related expenses, but the agent doesn't take your word for it. He claims all the deposits were unreported "income." Income from what? You work for a salary. But it's your word against his, and there is no "innocent until proven guilty" assumption in the eyes of the IRS. You appeal and lose, and you worry that a tax court may not rule in your favor. You settle and pay tax you don't owe on income you never had and pray to have this nightmare over with. Then the IRS tells you they want to look at other tax years you filed.... Now the ordeal starts all over for you. You have become the victim of a vicious system. Your crime was carelessness. Did all this have to happen? I imagine that psychiatrists who treat patients for post-audit trauma report the first question asked by the victims is: "Why me?"

THE IRS IS THIS COUNTRY'S LARGEST BUREAUCRACY —A GIANT WHOSE SOLE PURPOSE IS TO COLLECT MONEY

With close to 120,000 employees, the Internal Revenue Service is the largest agency of the U.S. Government. This should come as no surprise, considering that the IRS brings in total annual revenues of about a trillion dollars.

The Service is headquartered in Washington and is headed by a Commissioner who is appointed by the President. The country is divided into seven regions, each headed by an IRS Regional Commissioner, who is also a political appointee. There is a further division into 63 Districts, each headed by a Director. Then there are ten Service Centers (Fresno, Ogden, Austin, Philadelphia, Atlanta, Holtsville, Andover, Cincinnati, Memphis), where you send your tax return each year. It is at one of these Service Centers that the processing of your tax return—and potential trouble—begins.

The information in your return is keypunched for entry into the big IRS computer in West Virginia. Because of the large total number of returns filed each year (about 200,000,000—including individual, corporate, and other returns), the IRS has to hire many temporary workers as keypunch operators during the busiest time, from January through April. These operators are poorly trained, overworked, and paid minimum wage. Since they are tired and careless and have to process such a huge number of returns in limited time, many errors occur. As many as ten percent of all returns entered into the computer are in error because of the carelessness of the keypunch operators—and these errors by IRS employees do result in audits.[4]

Your return, possibly already in error, now goes into the central IRS computer in West Virginia. The computer is central to all IRS activity. This fact cannot be overstated in trying to understand the mentality of the organization. Virtually everyone at the IRS, from the Commissioner down, worships The Computer—sometimes forgetting that people program the computer as well as enter data into it. The computer crashed in 1985, and by the IRS's own admission, many millions in tax revenue were lost forever.

The digital villain now starts to work on your return. The first thing the computer does is to check your Social Security number (SSN). The IRS identifies you not by name or any other means but by your SSN. If you (or the Service Center keypunchers) entered the wrong SSN for you or your joint filer or a dependent,

TEN PERCENT OF ALL RETURNS ARE ENTERED INCORRECTLY INTO THE IRS COMPUTER

A HUGE COMPUTER IS THE HEART OF THE ENTIRE IRS MACHINE

---

[4]Typically, errors of the type caused by keypuch operators result in mismatches of numerical information and are dealt with by mail. As of this year, however, the IRS will consider all such correspondence as audits. The mail contact audits may also lead to full- fledged examinations by the IRS.

the machine will catch the error and spew out your return for examination. Next, the computer looks for obvious things that computing machines were designed for—arithmetic errors.

An arithmetic error will also cause your return to be tagged for examination by an IRS employee, and usually you will then be contacted by mail to resolve the problem. An audit by mail is—usually—not a big deal, as you can resolve the mathematical error with the IRS quickly and without adversity. Some even say that an arithmetic error reduces your chance for a "real" audit as it tags your return and kicks it out of the system for some time, but I know of no actual proof of this theory.

NEVER FILE A RETURN REPORTING "NICE" ROUNDED NUMBERS

A related issue is the "nice-numbers trap." If the IRS employee who looks at your return once it has been identified by the computer sees expenses or other numbers that look "too nice to be real": $15,000, or $29,000 (rather than: $14,987.56, or $28,759.12, for example), then this suspicion may result in an audit. It should be noted that while most audits are indeed triggered by the computer, a small percentage of all audits (about five percent) are caused by other factors. One of these factors is information provided to the IRS by people who claim to have knowledge about your financial life.

The next step in the computer check is a matching program. Here all the financial information that is reported about you from institutions and employers on forms 1099 and W-2 is matched against what you have reported yourself on the return. Any mismatched information will cause your return to be pulled out by the computer for an audit, at least by mail.

Assuming you have passed all these tests by the computer, your return now faces the big IRS acid test: the Discriminant Function (which the IRS abbreviates as "DIF"). Here the computer constructs your statistical profile. What is this statistical profile, and why is it needed? In theory, the principle is as follows. The IRS does not know whether or not you paid your taxes to the full extent of the law, or whether you cheated. So it wants to compare you, statistically, with the group of people it believes cheat on their taxes. If you look, statistically, like the people in that group (that is, you have an income level similar to theirs, and you have deductions in the same categories and in similar proportions to the "bad guys," and you have other characteristics in common with them, such as your profession)—then, chances are, you cheat as well. Therefore, goes the IRS logic, you too should be audited. This is the IRS reasoning that underlies the entire process and presumes your guilt even before an actual examination begins!

Are you guilty or not? In many cases, nobody knows for sure whether a person cheated on his or her taxes. Why? The following fact should be quite convincing. Every year, Money magazine asks a group of 50 top tax experts to prepare the return of a hypothetical individual, and they then publish the comparison of the experts' results. In all the years this has been done, not a single time have even two of the experts agreed on the exact amount of tax due! This example, as well as inherent vagueness in the thousands of pages of tax law, court rulings and precedents, shows that it is virtually impossible to say whether or not an actual individual pays the full amount of tax due. (Note that here we are not talking about criminal cases, tax evasion and fraud.)

What is the reality then? The IRS doesn't know (or even care) whether or not you cheated—they are simply concerned with one issue: can we get more money from this individual? And this is the key to the Secret Formula, the DIF. The IRS has past records of people whose audits resulted in additional tax due (actually the information is based on results of the notorious Taxpayer Compliance Measurement Program, discussed later). The DIF, then, is a rule that discriminates between those people from whom the IRS was able in the past to squeeze more money in audits, and those from whom the IRS could not get more money. The DIF contains variables that are based on your income, your expenses, your deductions. If the combination of factors in the formula makes you look like a potential milking cow for more tax dollars, the IRS will audit you.

A large percentage (ten percent or more) of all individual returns are selected for audit by the DIF. Once this happens, IRS employees (Classifiers/Screeners) manually scan the returns tagged by the computer, and audits actually occur for fifteen percent or more of the returns selected by the machine. This fact—that only some percentage of the DIF-selected returns are actually

THE DIF
IS THE
COMPUTER
FORMULA THAT
LOOKS FOR
RETURNS OF
TAXPAYERS WHO
—
STATISTICALLY
—
YIELD MORE
MONEY WHEN
AUDITED

audited—will be quite useful for us later on in constructing audit-proofing strategies.

Let's return to the IRS system. If you were not selected for an audit, the IRS continues processing your return. If you owe taxes your check will be cashed rather quickly, and if you are due a refund, one will be sent to you. If you are selected for an audit, your file is sent to your local District Office. The Examination Division in the District Office will then contact you, usually by letter, for an Office Audit. Or a Field Audit may be conducted at your place of business or residence. The District Office also has a Collection Division, responsible for getting the money from you following an audit, a Criminal Investigation Division, and a Problem Resolution Office. In the next chapter we discuss how the people of the IRS view you, the taxpayer.

CHAPTER 3

HOW THE IRS VIEWS YOU, THE TAXPAYER

There is an old Yiddish joke about the guy who comes home and cheerfully tells his wife "Honey, the doctor examined me thoroughly and found nothing wrong! I'm as healthy as can be." "What?" says his wife, "Surely he didn't examine you well enough, or else he would have found something wrong with you!"

In the eyes of the IRS, there is something wrong with all of us taxpayers. The mission of the IRS is to find out just what it is. This notion is clearly stated in the official Internal Revenue Manual:[5]

> It has been indicated that, where a regular or normal tax examination ends, an in-depth examination should begin.

Or, in other words: believe no one! Search hard enough and you will find something. Other official IRS guidelines to its agents describe methods of putting the audited individual on the defensive, using intimidation and psychological pressure, and pursuing the case until weaknesses eventually appear, which can then be exploited for more money. The IRS is able to assume you are guilty because you are not (at least not yet) accused in court of

---

[5] *Internal Revenue Manual*, Section 4325, 132-1 (4-11-80).

having committed a crime, which would give you the benefit of the assumption of innocence until proven guilty in the eyes of the law.

THE IRS VIEWS EVERY SINGLE TAXPAYER AS A POTENTIAL TAX CHEATER

This is a very tricky point. The IRS always assumes that you are guilty of something, and the auditor tries to find that "something." In fact, the actual reason for the computer's having chosen you for an audit is not known to the auditor! The whole process is a Kafkaesque nightmare. You stand accused of something unknown to you—even unknown to your tormentors!

Usually, however, the audit process does not lead to criminal charges. Understand that the IRS is generally interested in one thing: more dollars. It will try to get these dollars from you by depriving you of any tax deduction it can. In some cases, IRS employees will even use the implied or actual threat of criminal charges to get you to admit to owing more money. Few audits result in criminal charges of tax evasion and fewer result in prison sentences. But the threat is definitely there.

THE KEY TO IRS EFFECTIVENESS IS INSTILLING FEAR IN ALL OF US

The IRS has been cultivating this atmosphere of fear for many decades. Ironically, much of the success of the IRS in spreading fear among us taxpayers is due to one individual who was not even employed by the IRS: the gangster Al Capone. Since the successful conviction of the elusive Al Capone for tax evasion 50 years ago, the IRS has enjoyed an almost legendary aura. However innocent we may be, somewhere in the backs of our minds is the common fear (rational or otherwise) of being caught in the clutches of the IRS and ending up in jail.

Since the social upheavals of the 1960s, however, this instinctive, implanted fear of the great Goliath has been on the decline. The IRS has noticed an increasing boldness on the part of the taxpayer and realized the need for new "examples." It began an active search for scapegoats. It wanted someone who was well-known, generally disliked by the public, and who would be convicted of tax evasion in a court of law and given a stiff sentence that would then serve to instill renewed fear in the public. After a concentrated research effort, the IRS found exactly what they were looking for in the person of Leona Helmsley. The immensely wealthy, arrogant, and oft-despised Queen of Mean, as she has been called, fit the bill very well. The government was able to prove that Helmsley was guilty of tax evasion because she fraudulently deducted over a million dollars in renovation expenses for her home, rather than for her hotels as she had claimed on her tax return. She was sentenced to jail in a much-publicized trial. As if to make sure that we all paid attention, in the following years since the Helmsley trial, several other wealthy, although less-known, people were sentenced to jail for tax evasion in trials that were extensively covered by the media. The doctrine of fear was on its way back. Even the President is not safe from the long arm of the IRS, as we know from news reports about Mr. Clinton's alleged underpayment of taxes many years ago.

In the eyes of the IRS we are all guilty of something. Depending on what it is that the IRS thinks we do to avoid paying our debt to the government, it classifies us taxpayers into three main categories: nonfiler, underreporter, overdeductor.

NONFILER

A "nonfiler" as the IRS refers to him or her, is a person who has not filed a tax return for at least one tax year. Not filing a tax return when tax is due is a crime and can lead to felony charges and jail sentences. The IRS uses computer matching techniques to catch nonfilers. If you earn wages or work as an independent contractor, documents filed with the IRS (forms 1099, W-2) will be matched against your social security number and you will be caught. Only rare individuals—for example, an undocumented illegal alien who earns a living in cash—can escape detection for a while. Even such a person will eventually be caught by other means. The IRS estimates that about three percent of the population are nonfilers; others believe the figure is somewhat higher.

UNDERREPORTER

"Underreporter" is how the IRS refers to a person who reports on his or her return an income that is smaller than the actual one. The underreporter is, by far, the greatest obsession of the IRS. A nonfiler is someone who doesn't report at all and can eventually be caught and made to pay up. However, those of us who do report an income to the IRS are all underreporters in the eyes of the Service. The greatest percentage of IRS effort concentrating on people who do file is aimed at proving underreported income.

The underreporter is the government's worst taxpaying enemy. The IRS knows that in many situations it is easy to conceal income. This leads to the IRS' belief that all of us do it, and that if they shake you hard enough, you will reveal to them the sources of your hidden income.

The ideal underreporter could be someone who lives in a small community practicing a barter economy. A fisherman living in Alaska gives a local artist some fish, and she, in turn, gives him a painting. No cash was transferred, no transactions recorded, and (unless someone reports them to the IRS) no one will be the wiser and this trade and its implicit incomes will forever remain untaxed.

Close to this kind of underreporter is the person who deals solely (or almost solely) in cash. Cash transactions, like barters, are almost impossible to detect. Large transactions ($10,000 or more) must be documented under government requirements, but smaller ones are not reported. Ironically, your friendly neighborhood bank is your worst enemy. Banks report interest income to the IRS. Also, as our introductory story shows, banks can be made to reveal all of your transactions. If you made money in cash but put it in your bank account, the IRS can trace the deposit. So even if your deposit was not income but of any of a million other kinds, the insatiable Goliath will claim it was income if it traces your deposit ("everyone hides income"), and charge you additional tax, interest, and penalty.

Our economy is based on bank transactions, checks, electronic transfers, credit cards, and it is moving ever faster in this direction toward a perfect recording of all your financial transactions. The information superhighway is an excellent snooping tool for the IRS. In fact, the government is already pushing for the implementation of electronic devices (Clipper Chips) that will automatically decode and enable reporting of all electronic information traffic on computer networks to government agencies: the FBI, the CIA, and, yes, the IRS. Ostensibly, this cause is championed to help the government fight crime, especially drug deals, by making large cash transactions visible. In reality, the IRS will benefit the most from this electronic spying.

While making our economy more efficient, electronic filing systems, banks, credit card companies, and ATMs all help the IRS because transactions can be scrutinized easily. Many other countries have economies based much more on cash. It is common in such countries to see people leaving a bank with a huge wad of money in their hands, made possible by lower crime rates. In some of these countries as much as 60% of the economy is unreported to the government. Many people in Greece, Italy, Turkey and other countries are extensive underreporters or nonfilers. Our modern, technologically-advanced economy makes it difficult to underreport and at the same time puts honest people under suspicion of having unreported income by tracing transactions that may not necessarily be income.

Recent information indicates that the IRS believes that this country, too, has a vast underground economy, and that it now plans to go after this sector.[6] Ironically, the agency admits that it has no idea where to start looking. In fact, the IRS is so frustrated in trying to locate hidden income that this year it will initiate the use of a new kind of audit it is borrowing from its Criminal Investigations Division. This audit is called an Economic Reality Audit. The audits will concentrate on lifestyle variables. The IRS will try to conclude that you make more money than you declared, and thus have hidden income, if they can't reconcile your reported income with what they consider a higher lifestyle.

The IRS is so concerned with its hunt for hidden income that its agents will sometimes even overlook tax deductions (our next topic) that look inflated, because they are really looking for the mythical treasures of hidden income.

OVERDEDUCTOR

The overdeductor is someone who deducts against income more expenses, losses, charitable contributions or other deductions than he or she is entitled to. High deductions figure prominently in the Secret Formula and trigger many audits. The agent conducting the audit will try to challenge the legitimacy of deductions and

---

[6] *Tax Week*, June 30, 1995, p.2.

credits against income and will force you to give evidence to support every item. This evidence is usually in the form of receipts and other substantiation. Once you are the subject of an audit, however, more effort will still be spent on looking for invisible, unreported income.

Finally, a few words are in order about what may very well be the ugliest practice of the IRS. Like the Spanish Inquisition of the Middle Ages, the IRS encourages and actively seeks denunciations. Incredible as it may seem, the IRS will take an estranged wife's word against her husband, a husband's against his wife, a child's against his or her parents, as well as snitching by disgruntled employees or acquaintances.

THE IRS WILL REWARD ANYONE WHO WILL BETRAY YOU TO THEM

There is a special telephone number for conveying information to the IRS, and rewards are offered to anyone who will provide information leading to the collection of additional tax, in the form of a percentage of the amount collected. This practice opens the door to abuse and revenge by anyone who may hold a grudge against you. For this reason you should never discuss your taxes in casual conversation. You never know how others may view what you are saying, and what their own motives and agendas may be.

CHAPTER 4

BAD ECONOMICS AND BAD SCIENCE: HOW THE IRS DOES ITS RESEARCH

In the fall of 1943, the Germans moved into the Tuscan hill town of Santa Vittoria. The area had been controlled by the Nazis for some time but except for stationing a few military liaison personnel in town, the occupiers let the inhabitants go about their daily lives. New information from a secret source in town, however, indicated that the inhabitants were hiding from their German occupiers over a million bottles of the valuable local vermouth at an undisclosed location. The military vehicles carrying several hundred soldiers into town that morning were part of an operation aimed at finding this treasure.

After the usual gentle persuasion methods failed, the Germans decided on a more extreme measure. They would randomly select a few townsfolk for a thorough investigation. These people would be tortured until they revealed the location of the town's hidden bottles—the community's only wealth. On the appointed day, Nazi soldiers patrolled the near-empty streets and found what they thought was a random sample of three people. These were carried off to a nearby cave and never heard from again. The treasure, however, was never discovered.

What the Germans did not know was that the three people they captured were not random. They were fascists who had been kept under house arrest by the townspeople since before the bottles were hidden; thus they did not know the hiding place. On the day the Nazi selection was made, these three were let loose by the people while everyone else stayed at home. Santa Vittoria kept its treasure.

**THE TCMP
IS A POLICY
OF TORTURING
THE INNOCENT
TO GAIN
INFORMATION**

The IRS in modern-day America has a similar treasure-hunting scheme. It is called the Taxpayer Compliance Measurement Program (TCMP), and it's going to get even worse in the next few years.[7] Every three years, the IRS selects a purely random sample of taxpayers to be audited. Until recently, their numbers have been about 50,000. These poor souls are treated to what accountants refer to informally as "the audit from hell."

If you are among these people, selected for no reason but the bad luck of the draw, God help you. The IRS will not leave you alone. Auditors will want to see everything. This is the modern-day-American equivalent of being randomly chosen on the street for an endless session of torture when you have done absolutely nothing wrong. And your tormentors know that!

The TCMP audit will scrutinize your birth certificate, those of your family members, death certificates,

---

[7]As we go to press, however, the I.R.S.—aware of the criticism of the TCMP in this book and in my article in *Taxes* magazine (August 1995; see the Bibliography)—announced on October 23, 1995, that it is postponing indefinitely its planned TCMP effort originally scheduled to begin this month.

marriage or divorce certificates, every bank book you ever kept, every check you ever wrote, records of every bill you ever paid, slips for every credit-card charge you ever made, the list is endless. And what you will not find in your records you will be forced to obtain from institutions, at your expense and your loss of valuable time. No excuse will be accepted by the IRS, and nothing will ever get you out of this terrible ordeal until the Service decides that they are finished with you. This is one case where, while you have done absolutely nothing wrong, our modern, enlightened, human-rights-conscious system will offer you no protection whatsoever.

The TCMP is a government program of relentless pressure mounted against an innocent individual for the purpose of extracting statistical information about an entire society. What is truly amazing about this despicable misuse of statistics is that it is perfectly legal for our government do it. The IRS tries to use the information it obtains from the TCMP sample to uncover our collective treasure—more money in the form of additional tax to be reaped from future audits that will be based on the information extracted from the TCMP. Let us see how this is done.

NOTHING IS SACRED IN A TCMP AUDIT

The principle of statistical inference is a simple one. You can gain information about a very large population (even an "infinite" population, as statisticians refer to it) by selecting a random sample from the population and measuring some characteristic of interest. Election-year polls, as well as the many other polls reported in the media almost daily, demonstrate this principle. Polling organizations such as Gallup will often select a random sample of 1,000 people and find out how many people in the sample have a certain characteristic, say, an intention to vote for a particular candidate. The result of the survey of only 1,000 people or so can then be extended to the entire population using statistical inference. The polling organization will state that in the entire voting population, a given percentage will vote for the candidate, plus or minus some margin of error that will typically be 2 or 3 percent. Amazingly, even a relatively small sample of 1,000 people can reveal much information, and have a small margin of error when applied to the entire population. This is a remarkable fact and demonstrates the power of statistics and how it can be used effectively to gain information.

Exactly the same principle works in the TCMP. The IRS wants to learn about the taxpayer population. Since not every taxpayer can be examined (this would take forever and cost more than all audits would ever bring), a random sample is selected. In statistical terms, a sample of 50,000 taxpayers is huge. It is definitely much larger than would be required by modern statistical theory, and demonstrates the excesses of government and the very low value placed on our rights not to be harassed. But guess what: the IRS now plans to abuse statistics and us taxpayers even more. In 1995, the IRS has tripled the number of TCMP audits!

On the same interview on CNN in which she answered questions about this book (January 3, 1995), IRS Commissioner Margaret Milner Richardson also announced the IRS's plan to triple to 153,000 the number of audits of 1994 returns that will be chosen on a purely random basis—constituting the TCMP program.

The TCMP audit is exploratory, and as such it is costly to the government since it does not target individuals who can lead to additional tax revenues. Taxpayers have to pay for this IRS learning enterprise, and it is not at all clear that the investment is worth the cost. Recent research papers by the IRS's own statisticians demonstrate that the IRS is actually aware that this program is too expensive and that its scope should be curtailed.[8]

It is puzzling, therefore, that instead of decreasing the size of the random-audit program, the IRS plans to triple the number of the TCMP audits. Fifty-thousand such examinations were carried out on 1988 returns; 153,000 audits will be undertaken of 1994 returns.[9] The IRS first claimed that the cost of this program will be $225 million. In congressional hearings on Capitol Hill in July 1995, the IRS raised its estimate of the cost of this program to $550 million. If we include additional expenditures for processing, and the opportunity cost of

---

[8]"Using the Bootstrap to Reduce Sample Size in TCMP," by Chih-Chin Ho, *Proceedings of the American Statistical Association*, San Francisco, 1993.

[9]Note that of these 153,000 TCMP audits, 92,000 will be of individuals and the rest corporate and partnerships.

not auditing the kind of taxpayers known to yield more money, the TCMP program could cost taxpayers as much as a billion dollars.

What information could possibly be worth this sacrifice in taxpayer dollars at a time when reducing the deficit and cutting government costs are a national priority? The IRS already knows a lot about taxpayers from millions of past audits, TCMP or other. Over the years, the IRS has continuously developed and revised its discriminant function (DIF) tool for determining which kinds of taxpayers lead to additional revenues. One thing the IRS does not need is more exploratory audits. What the IRS needs instead are better research tools to analyze the millions of audited returns it already has, and to leave taxpayers free of the harassment of an unnecessary random audit.

The size of the sample the IRS proposes to use in its TCMP effort is not justified by any accepted statistical theory. In fact, on another CNN interview in April 1995, I strongly criticized the magnitude of the proposed program.[10] In searching for any possible statistical reasons for this unbelievably large random audit extravaganza the IRS was planning, I talked with a number of the most prominent statisticians of our time. With one exception,

---

[10]CNN Business News story aired throughout the day on April 7, 1995, and on the program "Your Money," on April 8 and April 9, 1995; also aired on CNN International. As always, the program's producer David Saltman was quick to recognize the importance of this story long before it was discovered by the other media when the congressional hearings on the TCMP started in Washington in July 1995.

all of them expressed the same outrage at this senselessly large sample size of 153,000. They could not justify it in any way and some even suggested that the reason must not be statistics, but rather intimidation. The only exception was a statistician who had done some consulting work for the IRS. He refused to criticize the agency.

As sample sizes increase, the value of additional information decreases—a manifestation of the law of diminishing returns (see Figure 1). The IRS learns a lot more about taxpayer behavior from the first 1000 audits it carries out than it does from the last 1000 audits. Thus having audited 50,000 taxpayers (in itself an excessively large number), the value of continuing to sample 100,000 more is dubious at best since the reduction in statistical error resulting from the additional 100,000

Figure 1: The Value of Information Obtained By Sampling

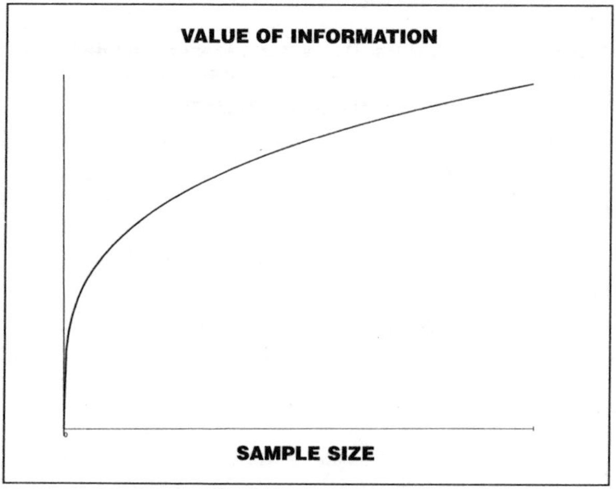

VALUE OF INFORMATION

SAMPLE SIZE

audits is minuscule. This is evident in Figure 2, which shows how sampling errors decrease with sample size. The effort is certainly not worth the cost when we consider both the value of information gained from sampling and the cost of the sample audits. Using very large sam-

Figure 2: Sample Size and Sampling Error

SAMPLE SIZE	SAMPLING ERROR PROPORTIONAL TO:
100	10%
1,000	3%
4,000	1.5%
10,000	1.0%
50,000	0.4%
150,000	0.3%

Figure 3: The Net (After-Costs) Gain From Sampling

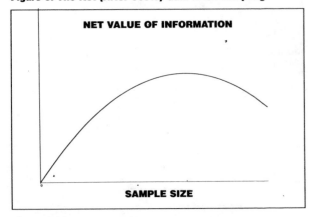

NET VALUE OF INFORMATION

SAMPLE SIZE

ples results in a net economic loss. This is demonstrated in Figure 3, which shows how costs of large samples can overrun the economic benefit of the information gained from the sampling. In other words, once you have audited enough people, if you have to pay for randomly auditing an additional 100,000 people, your gain in precision will not lead to enough tax revenues resulting from a better DIF to pay for these additional random audits. The effort will result in a net waste of money.

The loss to the economy of an excessive audit effort by the government is even greater when we consider what the TCMP audits do to productive taxpayers. Such audits can take a very long time (according to the IRS, the average could be over 44 weeks) and are extremely disruptive. Based on the size of the planned sample of random audits, the damage would be the equivalent of a medium-sized U.S. city having its economy grind to a standstill for a period of weeks. This translates into a significant loss in the nation's productivity.

And the costs and economic loss do not consider the unnecessary pain to honest taxpayers caught in this random web. According to the IRS, less than five percent of all taxpayers cheat. An in-depth, exhaustive audit of 153,000 random taxpayers will therefore represent unnecessary and lengthy harassment of more than 145,000 innocent people. What is the logic behind such an outrage? The nation's largest bureaucracy believes that bigger is always better. If more people are to be randomly audited, their logic goes, more information will be

**THE IRS
OVERUSES
RANDOM
AUDITING OF
INNOCENT
TAXPAYERS,
MAKING
TAXPAYERS
PAY FOR
UNNECESSARY
HARASSMENT**

available, and the information will somehow lead to more tax dollars. Costs, apparently, have not been figured into this formula. And neither has the IRS's antiquated discriminant function methodology, long superseded by modern routines requiring fewer data and giving higher accuracy. What the IRS plans to do is tantamount to performing exploratory surgery with stone-age tools where an X-ray would do. And the IRS already has many previous X-rays from past audit programs. Perhaps the threat of surgery is the real motive here: the belief that a horrendous random audit hanging over taxpayers might keep them in tow. When asked to respond to my criticism of the TCMP effort on CNN, Commissioner Milner Richardson replied: "We do it to enhance our compliance program, and taxpayers who file accurate returns, who keep good books and records should have nothing to fear." Apparently the Commissioner has not undergone a TCMP audit. Here is how *The New York Times* described one victim's ordeal:[11]

> Given the choice between another compliance audit and a root canal, said Mrs. Smith, who now works for an association of state tax officials, she would visit her dentist. Mrs. Smith, a former sports columnist, said that an IRS auditor even suggested digging up her backyard to see if she had not reported money earned writing freelance articles, which he said might have been secreted in cash in coffee cans.

---

[11]"IRS Is Preparing a Tough Audit for Groups of Unwary Taxpayers," by David Cay Johnston, *The New York Times*, July 19, 1995, front page.

CHAPTER 5

BATTLE OF THE STATISTICIANS

The breakdown of the random sample into two groups is achieved by a discriminant function (DIF). The very thorough audit of the sample of 50,000 or 150,000 unfortunate souls is supposed to reveal the information on income, deductions, expenses, losses, and contributions that the IRS believes will discriminate between the honest, fully-tax-paying people and the people who hide their income and overstate their deductions. Each piece of information is coded as a variable in the discriminant function, and the computer then searches for the combination of variables that will achieve the best possible discrimination between the two groups. The IRS makes no secret of its use of a "secret formula" to determine audits. Publicizing this very fact is yet another tool to intimidate us taxpayers. Here is Big Brother, spying on us with his secret formula that will tell him right away who's been naughty and who's been good. The IRS even implies that the secret formula, the DIF, is a very "complicated" equation that contains all kinds of information about us and can reveal what we do very accurately. My results of the analysis of a large sample of audited and unaudited returns paints a different picture. The number of significant variables in the IRS's DIF is probably relatively small. My study revealed that a handful of variables, all of them ratios, account for 90% of all the audits.

DISCRIMINANT ANALYSIS IS SUPPOSED TO SEGMENT THE POPULATION INTO TWO GROUPS: ONE BELIEVED TO BE HONEST, THE OTHER TAX-EVADING

Once the IRS completes the TCMP analysis, the rule it extracts from the discriminant analysis becomes, by the principles of statistical inference, the actual Secret Formula of the IRS, the DIF used in determining all future audits. Long before the IRS actually sees your return, they have already made up their minds—based solely on the characteristics of other people—whether they will let your claims stand as they are, or doom you to an audit. They've got your number!

From a statistical point of view, the DIF is not the most sophisticated program available today and it makes big errors for a variety of technical reasons. Discriminant analysis was developed in 1936 by the great British statistician Sir Ronald A. Fisher (1890-1962), as a statistical classification method. The technique requires particular assumptions, such as a normal distribution. In the case of the IRS, many of the underlying assumptions are severely violated. For one thing, none of the variables the IRS uses are normally distributed. For another, over the years the IRS has distorted the discriminant procedure in its pursuit to adapt it to tax audits. As far back as 15 years, consulting statisticians have recommended the IRS replace the discriminant analysis procedure (developed before computers) with a more modern technology, but to no avail.

The pure statistical method, derived from theory, requires the discriminant score to be a number between -1 and 1, negative numbers implying membership in one group ("audit"), and positive ones in the other ("no audit"). In their frenzy to computerize and to capitalize on as many pieces of information as possible, IRS statisticians have changed the discriminant procedure so much that now it doesn't even resemble the original, correct method. It is now a *quantitative* classification rather than a qualitative one (audit-no audit). What they do is to use (*misuse*) the DIF so it will give every taxpayer an actual *score*. This score is then used similarly to the old draft lottery. All taxpayers are rank-ordered by their DIF-scores from largest to smallest and the allotted number of audits for the year is obtained by counting down from the top—the highest DIF-score—to the lowest. The statistical underpinnings for this procedure are dubious at best.

From a *moral* point of view, however, the procedure is an utter disgrace. You have done nothing wrong, but you happen to be a physician. Or a waiter/waitress, or a building contractor, or a professor. Your occupation alone can give you a high DIF score. Add to this the usual expenses and other characteristics that go with your line of work, and chances are you will be audited. And you'll have to pay.

Discriminant analysis (in its original, undistorted form) is also used by banks to determine whether you are to be classified as a "good" or a "bad" credit risk. If you are classified as bad, you will be denied a loan. Recent litigation has challenged banks' use of this analysis as unfair, but don't try to complain to the IRS about using its DIF.

YOU MAY BE AUDITED AGAIN AND AGAIN JUST BECAUSE THE COMPUTER THINKS YOU LOOK LIKE SOMEONE WHO MIGHT UNDERPAY INCOME TAX

In this crucial drive to extract billions in extra revenues, the IRS has a very large division of statisticians to do battle with us all. The division is called Statistics of Income (SOI). The SOI employs people whose main purpose is to find ways of identifying those of us who can be squeezed for more dollars once our returns are examined.

The DIF: Revenue-Maximizing Tool or Adversarial Game-Strategy?

According to the von Neuman Theory of Games, which governs phenomena such as competition in the market place, economic behavior, as well as military strategies and a host of other conflict situations, the best strategy against an intelligent adversary is a random one. This immediately implies secrecy. The adversary should not be able to guess your strategy. In dealing with taxpayers using an ostensibly secret formula, the IRS accentuates the adversarial nature of its relationship with taxpayers and casts the tax-filing process as an antagonistic game played between the government and each citizen. Statements by IRS personnel to the media that they "tinker with the DIF every year, so it's never the same," further reinforce the image of the secret formula as a game-strategy tool designed to fool the enemy and keep us taxpayers on our toes.

In reality, however, the DIF is neither a randomly chosen strategy nor something that changes significantly from year to year. The reason is that if the DIF did indeed change much and if it were chosen to "fool" the taxpayer rather than for its real purpose, it would be ineffective. In actuality, the DIF is a statistically-derived rule designed to maximize the IRS's net gain from audits. A random, or changeable, strategy would always be less than optimal in this sense. This is why there are relatively few audits of simple tax returns and many more audits among people with complicated returns. A random strategy or one that changes from year to year would be more uniform among all classes of taxpayers. The DIF is a revenue maximizing tool—at least in its aims—but the IRS wants to make taxpayers think that it is more of the classic adversarial "you'll never know what I am going to do next" type of device.

The theory behind all this madness is a cynical one. Remember that by far the greatest obsession of the IRS is with hidden income. Truly hidden income is impossible to find. There is absolutely nothing on a taxpayer's return that would indicate directly the existence of hidden income. Hence the absurdity of the SOI operation. The division is on a constant statistical search for the perfect profile of the person who hides income. The main assumption is the following: Bad people hide income. Bad people are also greedy. Therefore, these people will not only hide their income, but they will also do other things—things that will be obvious to us from their tax returns. In addition to hiding their income, these people will also exaggerate their deductions and credits, making them easy to catch. Thus, the SOI statisticians are on a constant lookout for methods of find-

THE MAIN PURPOSE OF THE DIF IS TO MYSTERIOUSLY LEAD THE IRS TO THE TREASURES OF HIDDEN INCOME

ing these telltale signs on returns. The DIF is just the mechanism for searching for the signs.

Every year, the American Statistical Association holds its national meeting at a different location. These meetings are attended by many in the profession—mostly academics and statistical practitioners in business and industry. Here the state of the art is explored; new methods are presented and explained; and ideas are exchanged.

THE IRS STATISTICIAN CONTINUALLY LOOKS TO IMPROVE THE DIF

Every year, the SOI division of the IRS sends a disproportionately high number of its staff to flood these meetings. While academics and statisticians in industry present new papers with important results that expand the profession, the SOI people do not. They make minimal contributions to the meetings in the form of elementary presentations of obvious (and often incorrect) statistical uses. Their sole purpose in attending these meetings is to spy! These IRS spies infiltrate almost every one of the scores of parallel sessions conducted at the congress. They scout for new ideas from others, then go home to IRS headquarters and try to implement what they have learned by scavenging.

Most statisticians are honest, hard-working professionals. They naturally resent the blatant theft of their ideas by someone out to get them and the rest of us. Consequently, people attending the conferences tend not to talk to the dozens of IRS personnel buzzing around, considering them a nuisance. At one meeting, the session chair introduced the speaker from the IRS and joked: "She'll be taking your names and social security numbers, so don't leave the room...." Typically, when an IRS paper is presented, many other statisticians leave the room. Those who stay will almost always keep quiet and not ask questions or offer suggestions. The IRS personnel in each meeting room often circulate, aggressively asking others for advice on how to solve their statistical problems.

At one such meeting in San Francisco, an IRS statistician presented a paper: "Who Are the Nonfilers, and How Can We Catch Them?" The paper, included in a session that otherwise had interesting presentations by academics and industrial statisticians, stuck out like a sore thumb. It said nothing and consisted of a few transparent statements that all led to the same question: How can we, the IRS, use statistics to catch nonfilers? Here is a short excerpt:[12]

> ...SOI's ability to profile prior-year returns is based entirely on their being filed, processed and subject to sampling. In essence, SOI can only analyze "what comes in;" hence, it is necessary to note that SOI cannot measure the universe of "unknown" nonfilers *not in the system*. SOI can capture data on "unknown" nonfilers only after they file.

(Quotation marks and italics are all theirs.) The paper was part of the IRS's program called Compliance 2000,

---

[12]The paper was reprinted in the *Statistics of Income Bulletin*, Washington, DC: Internal Revenue Service, Summer 1993, p.55.

the purpose of which is to use statistics to "remove barriers to compliance" by the year 2000.

Then the presenter invited a discussion from the audience. Many people were offended and left the room in disgust, some making snide comments. Of those who remained, no one uttered a word. Finally one person raised his hand. With a thick British accent he went on to explain how the Inland Revenue Office in the U.K. catches nonfilers. The six IRS statisticians attending the session as well as the presenter all got out their notepads and feverishly started writing down everything that was said.

Generally less qualified and lower-paid than others, SOI statisticians need to improve continuously that dinosaur of a DIF and their other statistical implements, to make them more efficient for more and more audit-driven tax revenues. From the government's point of view, paying for these annual trips to conferences is a cheap way of trying to do the trick. But they get exactly what they pay for. In fact, another article in the same issue of the *SOI Bulletin* referred to above admits:

> Many government statistical agencies, including SOI, have not kept up with the explosive growth of statistical theory and methods.

It was at one such annual statistical meeting that the idea first struck me: statistics can be used both ways—by the government *and* by the taxpayer! I decided to use my own knowledge of statistics, which I believe to be far superior to that of the IRS statisticians, to do battle against them. I would use all the advanced methods at my disposal to counter the DIF. I will do so by using statistics to estimate the actual DIF, and I will give you the results.

CHAPTER 6

THE WHOLESALE APPROACH: A BUREAUCRACY GONE MAD

Recently, the IRS changed the definition of an "audit." The new definition includes correspondence by mail between the agency and the taxpayer as well as face-to-face encounters. The change was made, apparently, in order to show a statistically higher audit percentage and bring the total annual IRS audit rate to 2.21%.[13] This frantic scurry to audit increased numbers of people, and, more importantly, to *appear* to be auditing more people (some of them in the scary "random testing" TCMP type of examination) has a very good reason. The IRS is under siege. There are a number of new proposals in Congress to change the tax system. The move to a flat tax seems to be gaining support, and among the tax reform proposals now under study is one that suggests doing away with the IRS altogether. Even if the mildest reform plan is accepted, the IRS would never be the same: its powers would be curtailed and its size reduced.

The fear of reduced power explains IRS statements in the media about how many billions they have collected in the last few years, how many people they have audited, and, in the words of Commissioner Milner

---

[13]G. Guttman, "What is an Audit?," *Tax Notes*, December 19, 1994, p. 1462.

Richardson in the CBS News interview quoted earlier, that "[IRS audits are] clearly a good deal for the Government." The pressure to prove themselves is probably one reason for the IRS's plan to triple the size of the TCMP sample, since it is a high-profile item that can give the IRS the added bonus of increased taxpayer apprehension and, the IRS hopes, enhanced voluntary compliance. But as became clear during Congressional testimony by IRS personnel, a former Commissioner and a former Director of the agency, the IRS doesn't know where to look.

The most ambitious development of all, with the greatest potential for taxpayer abuse, is the new IRS audit strategy called the "Wholesale Approach," which was criticized during the Congressional hearings on the TCMP. This new direction defies all reason. The wholesale approach is based on a theory of market segmentation. For some crazy reason, the IRS has come to the belief that somewhere in America there is an entire segment of the taxpaying population that habitually fails to comply with the tax laws. Instead of tax cheaters being evenly distributed throughout the country, as any educated person might surmise, the IRS now believes that all tax cheaters are somehow congregated together. The question is: where? To answer this preposterous question, the IRS is willing to spend many billions in taxpayer dollars, audit countless numbers of people, and leave no stone unturned in its search.

The wholesale approach is a complete change in philosophy. The IRS's aim from now on is not to look for individuals to audit, but rather to look for a segment of the taxpayer population and to audit heavily in this segment. The agency hopes that if it could just concentrate enough resources on research, including artificial intelligence, it could somehow find the segment to be given this mega-audit: doctors making over $160,000, who drive Volvos, have at least two children, and have either blue or green eyes.... Or maybe their desired market segment consists of all single parents making no more than $40,000, who work two jobs and eat out no more than twice a week.

Whatever the IRS is thinking is blurred by the fear of the congressional axe. And, apparently, there is no depth to which the IRS is unwilling to stoop. Searching for the mythical segment of the population which will lead them to treasures beyond the wildest imagination, the IRS was apparently ready to violate the principles of individual privacy protected by the Constitution. In March 1995, the IRS announced that it "made a mistake" in a notice issued the previous December that implied that the IRS planned to conduct research by tapping into credit, financial, and real estate transaction records in order to study *broad groups of taxpayers*. The admission of the "mistake" followed a rash of taxpayer complaints about possible violation of taxpayers' rights to privacy and prompted reassurances from the IRS that they do not intend to identify specific individuals. The

IRS still plans to look at these private records of credit, financial, and real estate information, but (if you believe the IRS) they will not identify individuals for contact. They will, however, "look at the population of filers and break them down by market segment, putting them into homogenous groups, so we could better target compliance efforts."[14] Table 2 above is a reprint of an actual IRS document, "Appendix II, Table II.1," presented by the IRS to the Oversight Subcommittee of the House Ways and Means Committee at its July 18, 1995, meeting on the TCMP. This table should give you an idea about the "market segments" the IRS has in mind and about the number of taxpayers within each segment the agency wants to audit on TCMP. See which segment you fall into, and compute your chance of being randomly audited. Can you explain why some people have a much higher chance than others of winning the random-audit-and-not-'cause-you-did-anything-wrong lottery?

In the 1980s, the Securities and Exchange Commission (SEC) was successful in finding cheaters of a different kind, insider traders, by using a wholesale approach. The SEC was able to determine through extensive investigations, including scrutinizing private financial records, an entire segment of the Wall Street community involved in illegal insider trades. Now the IRS wants to cash in on this approach. But the reason for the SEC's success was that the insider traders—by the very nature of their crime—tended to use each other's

[14]IRS announcement, reprinted in *Taxes*, March 1995, p.149

TABLE 2: Market Segments and Sample Size for TCMP

Market Segment	Population of Segment	Sample Size
Farm Business	850	8,602
Building Trade Contractors	942	5,851
All Other Construction	226	6,049
Manufacturing	201	6,313
Mining and Minerals	28	3,457
Agricultural Services	233	3,067
Wholesale Trade	241	7,792
Direct Sales	187	1,595
Auto, Boat Dealers and Service Stations	149	3,965
Food and Beverage	342	4,931
Apparel, Furniture, and General Merchandise	130	3,540
Retail—All Other	295	4,268
Real Estate	312	5,759
Finance and Insurance	246	4,040
Air, Bus, and Taxi	75	2,805
Other Transportation, and Utilities	381	3,703
Amusement, Recreation, and Motion Pictures	194	3,671
Medical and Health	444	5,034
Business and Personal Services	509	6,144
Hotel, Lodging,and Automotive	813	5,473
Unable to Classify	57	15,317
Miscellaneous Business and Personal Services	532	2,382
Miscellaneous Services	465	5,496

THERE ISN'T A SHRED OF SCIENTIFIC EVIDENCE TO INDICATE THAT TAX CHEATERS CONGREGATE IN A "MARKET SEGMENT" WAITING TO BE DISCOVERED BY THE IRS

information, tended to work for investment banks, and shared other characteristics that made them a uniform group. Absolutely nothing of the sort can be said about tax cheaters. And how do we even define a tax "cheater"? What the IRS may consider cheating, someone may legitimately believe is simply aggressive interpretation of the tax law. Not a single sociological, psychological, or demographic study exists indicating that tax cheaters conveniently congregate somewhere. Let's all hope that the Congress can stop this madness before all our constitutional rights are violated.

CHAPTER 7

AN ADVERSARIAL RELATIONSHIP

The most important thing for you to remember when dealing with IRS agents is that they are not your friends, no matter what. By the very nature of the system, the IRS is out to get you, since it is a greedy bureaucracy with the sole purpose of collecting money. Horror stories surface from time to time about checks made out to third parties arriving by mistake at IRS processing centers and being altered and cashed by the agency, leaving their intended recipients to sue for reimbursement.

The IRS always interprets laws in its favor. The tax law consists of thousands of pages of legislation, rulings, and precedents. It is supposed to be fair to the taxpayer, but interpretations can vary widely. So, even if the law gives you a break on a particular item, it does not mean that the IRS will. Once the IRS agent looks at the particular issue in question, he or she will likely interpret the law in favor of the IRS. Often, there are IRS guidelines on how to handle various issues. Then, as a result of litigation, courts make provisions and interpret the law in a way that allows the taxpayer some latitude. In most cases, the auditor, who is usually a relatively low-level IRS employee, will not be aware of the court ruling that allows you to make use of some deduction to your advantage. At the audit, you will be left having to fight

A TAX AUDIT IS AN IRS GAME AIMED AT DEFEATING YOU

THE IRS WILL
ALWAYS
INTERPRET THE
LAW IN THE WORST
POSSIBLE WAY
FOR YOU

for your right to the deduction with a person who does not know the ruling and is not willing to allow you a wider interpretation. "I read this rule to mean that I don't have to capitalize these expenses over four years" may not convince the auditor who believes that you had to capitalize and therefore were entitled to a much smaller tax deduction for that year. You will have to find the particular statute or precedent allowing you to do what you did when you prepared your return.

The audit process is a thorough investigation of every line item. If there is any way at all that an issue can be interpreted in a way that leads to more dollars for the government, the agent will do so. At the end of the audit, the agent will give you his or her report including all the disallowances of your deductions that the agent believes result from the audit. Then you will have to fight for your rights first with the agent, then with his or her supervisor, an appeals officer, and possibly in court.

Don't be fooled by social graces or small talk or niceties. The IRS agent is not your friend. He or she is only interested in one thing: your money. Hang tight and don't give an inch. The agent is trained in psychological methods that are designed to intimidate you. The IRS manuals contain explicit instructions to their agents on how to make you uncomfortable, how to exert psychological pressure on you, and how to intimidate you. Everything is so by design. Nothing is casual even if it may seem so.

The agent will call you at home, often at inconvenient times such as 7 AM or worse. The agent will call you at work, exposing you to your employer or co-workers as someone who is being "audited by the IRS." The agent will meet you on his/her territory, where you will sit in a dark and stuffy room waiting for the agent to ask questions, demand explanations.

IRS strategy is designed to make you feel pushed, uncomfortable and ultimately admit that your claims and deductions were unreasonable. Maybe you will even reveal that hidden income they are after, and as a bonus give them that foreign bank account they know you have...and under threat of a criminal investigation agree to pay a lot more tax and interest and penalties and the agent will look good in the eyes of supervisors and eventually be promoted.

But also remember that the IRS agent is still human. As such, the agent has weaknesses just like you and I. The trick is, of course, to find those weaknesses and exploit them to your advantage. The auditor is trying to make an assessment: is this an honest person, or one who has hidden some income which I can find? The way to behave in such an encounter is to try to gain the agent's confidence.

This can be done by various methods, and is a tricky task. One tax attorney I know has an interesting habit. He tries to look over the auditor's shoulder at his or her calendar. If the calendar looks full, the agent is very busy and then one strategy will be used by the attorney: delay, be indirect, stretch things out.

AN IRS AUDIT IS DESIGNED TO MAKE YOU UNDOMOFRTABLE AND COMPLIANT

IF YOU CAN USE PSYCHOLOGY TO COUNTER ITS USE BY THE IRS AGENT

One tactic that seems to work is to ask a lot of questions: Why do you need this? What should I do in this situation? I thought this was a reasonable way to handle this issue, don't you? This strategy may throw off the auditor. He or she may also get tired of answering your questions and will want to get the examination over with.

LOOK FOR SUBTLE WEAKNESSES IN YOUR ADVERSARY, AND EXPLOIT THEM

Some IRS agents, especially the young, tend to be idealistic in some bizarre way: they believe that their mission is to educate you, the taxpayer. They want to teach you how to do your taxes correctly so that you will not be audited in the future (as if incorrect filing is what got you to them in the first place!). These auditors are easier to handle because they have a clear weakness. Here you should cater to the agent's desire to educate you. Ask questions on how you could do your taxes better in the future. "How can I learn from this experience so that next time I will not be audited?" or "I want to learn to prepare my taxes well." You will be surprised how far such an approach can get you with an agent bent on a mission of "educating" you about the tax system. Defer to such an agent and he or she may even forget what they are there for...if you're lucky.

CHAPTER 8

NEVER PANIC!

So you got that letter calling you for an audit by the IRS. The worst thing you can do is panic. Take some time to think. Don't act quickly. In fact, this is probably the best advice I can give you. Time is always on your side, even though time will cost you interest if you ultimately owe the government more tax. The IRS is under very tight time constraints. This fact cannot be over-emphasized. The audit process begins right after you file, when returns are entered into the IRS computer in West Virginia. The DIF starts to work immediately, spewing out identification codes for those returns selected for audit.

**THE TIME ELEMENT: THE IRS HAS
THREE YEARS FROM THE TIME YOUR RETURN IS DUE
(USUALLY APRIL 15) TO ASK FOR MORE TAX**[15]

The time line of the audit game is shown in Figure 4.

This means that if you filed your 1995 return on April 15, 1996, the government must finish the audit

---

[15]There are some important exceptions. If the IRS determines that you have not declared 25% or more of your income, they have six years to complete your audit. Also, if you are a nonfiler, then since there was no date of filing, they have no date for completing your investigation! They can take forever.

Figure 4: The time line of the audit game

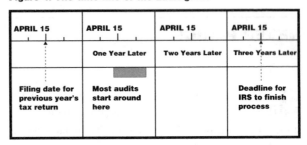

APRIL 15	APRIL 15	APRIL 15	APRIL 15
	One Year Later	Two Years Later	Three Years Later
Filing date for previous year's tax return	Most audits start around here		Deadline for IRS to finish process

by April 15, 1999, to ask for additional tax. This may seem like a very long period of time. In effect, it is quite short. Anyone experienced in the incredibly inefficient bureaucracy of the U.S. government will recognize this fact. While a proficient private accountant could complete an audit of your entire tax return in a single afternoon, the same return can take an IRS agent 6 months, a year, or even more to conclude. A recent IRS publication on "Taxpayer Burden in the IRS" states that the average elapsed time in examination in 1990 was 44 weeks.[16] There are many reasons for this unfathomable inefficiency. First of all, the IRS agent is neither as qualified nor as motivated as a private accountant. And IRS agents are typically very overworked. They are 9-to-5 types who have to conduct a certain number of audits in a given period of time. They have little incentive to do a good job, work overtime, or be efficient at what they do.

---

[16]"Mean Elapsed Time in Examination" a display in a paper "Measuring Taxpayer Burden," by IRS statisticians, *Proceedings of the American Statistical Association*, San Francisco, 1993.

While the IRS system is itself computerized, the agents are not. An experiment in training the agents in the use of personal computers a few years ago was declared a complete failure. The agents remain pencil-and-paper people, who take their time looking at your file, misplacing it, working on another file for a while, going on to yet a third file, calling in sick, and attending training meetings. If you are lucky, they may even lose your file or misplace it for an extended period of time and pass their deadline of three years from the time you filed. Then you are home free. Even the most efficient and dedicated agent may take several months to complete an audit of your return. If they make a mistake, if they are stalled long enough, if they lose your file—you gain from it, and may be off the hook completely.

There is another, rather touchy point about time. Audits are usually initiated 14 to 17 months after you have filed your return. If the audit is taking longer than the agent expected and the deadline is approaching, the IRS may request that you sign an extension consent form. Usually, the requested extension is for six more months beyond the deadline (Form 872), although the IRS may request that you sign an indefinite extension (Form 872-A). What happens here is that the IRS admits that they have been slow and inefficient in conducting the audit of your return and that all the time they had (three years from the time you filed!) was still not enough for them. Therefore, they now want you to give up your constitutional right to have this horrendous process over within

REMEMBER, TIME IS ON YOUR SIDE: WELCOME ANY DELAY AND LOOK FOR ANY EXCUSE TO ASK FOR POSTPONEMENTS

reasonable time. Personally, I never give up my rights, and I don't think that you should either. While the laws should be fair to the taxpayer, most of the tax law system favors the IRS and is designed to increase government revenues. Few laws are there to protect the citizen from abuse by the all-powerful IRS. The law limiting the time the IRS has to collect money from you is, therefore, almost an exception. It is a small provision designed to protect you from being harassed forever by the agency.

There is a trick, however, that allows the IRS to abuse its powers against you and to help them make you give up your right to end the process—in case you haven't guessed. The IRS will use the following reasoning to pressure you to sign away your rights: We need more time to check your claims and deductions, so that we can allow them to stand. As they are right now, we will have to disallow them. If you give us the time we need by signing the extension form, we will use the time for this purpose. If you don't sign, we will disallow all deductions that we had no time to check. This incredibly warped logic is consistent, however, with the IRS being all-powerful and your having no defense against them. It sits well with the assumption that you are guilty until you prove you are innocent. This practice amounts to official blackmail. The IRS uses it daily. If this request is made of you, you will have to make a difficult choice. Sometimes delaying the decision to sign or not sign the extension may get you over the problem, because in the meantime the deadline may have slipped by. In such a case, you win everything—there will be no assessment. But more often, the IRS agent will be aware of the need to have the extension form signed before the deadline arrives and will pressure you to sign. As a rule, never sign the indefinite extension form, Form 872-A. If the auditor asks you to sign it, argue that you do not see why he or she would need an indefinite extension, and that one for six more months should be more than enough (Form 872).

You should try your best not to sign the limited extension, if you can. It often happens that once you sign Form 872, the audit will continue and eventually the inefficient snail-paced auditor will again ask you to sign an extension for another six months.... Once you are dragged into the cycle of giving up your rights to allow the excesses of the IRS to continue, you may be a lost soul, forever to be audited. Such extended audits can last for years! The best tactic is to be evasive. Outright refusal to sign the form may not be in your best interest. The auditor may simply make good on the threat and assess you in the worst possible way as your punishment for not signing away your rights. You could still appeal, but you will be one step behind in this difficult game. As is the case in most situations dealing with the IRS, indirect, evasive strategies are best.

So in any case (leaving out the fact that interest may be accruing), time is on your side. Take your time. If the letter gives you 30 days to respond to the audit request, take 30 days. Use the time to work out a strategy. Look

THE IRS WILL TRY TO PUSH YOU TO GIVE UP YOUR RIGHT TO HAVE THE AUDIT FINISHED WITHIN THE LEGAL TIME LIMIT. RESIST THE PRESSURE!

THE IRS AUDIT IS A COMPREHENSIVE SEARCH FOR INFORMATION— EVIDENCE THAT YOU UNDERPAID YOUR TAX over all your records and compile the information the IRS has requested. Obtain copies of missing records, such as misplaced bank statements, etc.

NEVER GIVE THE IRS AGENT ANY INFORMATION HE OR SHE HAS NOT ASKED FOR.

The agent follows the IRS priorities: first look for any hidden income; second, look for deductions that cannot be fully substantiated. So don't help the IRS do its work. Give an agent no information unless he or she asks for it. Be as tight-lipped as you possibly can. It is a crime punishable by law to lie to the IRS. However, evasive answers such as "I will get back to you on this later," are not a crime. Delay, take your time, think, give no additional information.

A third element on your side—and most definitely the most important one—is your brain. If you bought this book, chances are you are more intelligent than your typical IRS agent. Use your brain! You are engaged in a battle for your dollars against a stubborn, vicious adversary. Take your time, compose yourself, and try to answer as little as possible. Time is on your side, you control much of the information the IRS receives, and you can use your wits in the battle against them. If you play your hand well, you may win the IRS audit game.

BEWARE OF THE IRS TRYING TO ENTRAP YOU: BE CAREFUL ANSWERING QUESTIONS

In case you are suspected of criminal tax evasion or criminal nonfiling of returns, the above advice is even more important. The IRS agents are trained in entrapping you. In many ways, they operate outside the law. They will give you no Miranda rights, and will ask you "Catch 22" questions that will entrap you either way you answer. For example, if you did not file a tax return and the agent asks you: "Did you file your tax return for 1995?" you lose any way you answer. If you answer: "No," you just admitted to the crime of non-filing. If you answer "Yes," when in fact you did not file, you just lied to the IRS, which is an even worse crime. Both are punishable by law and may result in prison terms. The only right answer in this case is no answer at all, something like: "I will get back to you after I consult my accountant (attorney)."

Panic may take different forms. Some people freak out when they get The Letter. To avoid having to go through the terrifying experience themselves (and often also feeling their time is too valuable to be wasted in an audit) these people hire a tax lawyer or accountant to go in for them. This may be a mistake. Assuming you prepared your own return, no one else knows your tax situation as well as you do. No one else can explain certain expenses, deductions, losses, credits the way you can. Trust someone else to do the job and indeed you will not have to face the IRS agent. But on the other hand, in addition to paying high attorney or accountant fees, you may also pay more tax as a result of the audit than if you faced the enemy yourself. Additionally, tax attorneys and tax accountants are agents hired on your behalf. Your best interest may not always be their best interest. These professionals deal with the IRS on a daily basis. They have a strong incentive not to burn any bridges, not to antagonize anyone, and to maintain friendly relations with IRS personnel. For the sake of a future relationship with the IRS, your hired agent may be willing to sacrifice some of your interests now. This is only true of the less professional tax preparers and attorneys. There is a wide variety of tax practitioners out there. Some are excellent, others are less qualified or interested. I have met some practitioners who would stop at nothing to protect their clients from the IRS. They actually feel the pain of the audit victim and will spend time and effort on behalf of their client against the IRS. Some of these professionals are more concerned with trying to avoid audits for their clients than they are with making more money, or with trying to be nice to the IRS. Find such a professional, if you decide that you need one. Use the same principle you would use in finding a doctor: look for the best.

IF YOU CHOOSE TO HIRE A TAX PROFESSIONAL, LOOK FOR THE BEST

There are situations where you need a tax practitioner. You also need to understand the difference between the two types of tax professionals: attorneys, and accountants. An attorney may not be as well versed in accounting, but should know the law better than an accountant, so if you are in serious trouble with the IRS, for example, if you are under investigation by the Criminal Investigations Division (CID), you probably need an attorney. Attorneys are bound by attorney-client privilege, which means that if they find that you did something wrong they can not be forced to reveal such "privileged" information to the IRS, or to anyone. If you have a serious accounting problem with your return, without legal complications, you may need to hire an

BE AWARE THAT YOUR BEST INTEREST AND THAT OF THE TAX PROFESSIONAL REPRESENTING YOU MAY NOT ALWAYS COINCIDE

accountant to help your case with the IRS. Accountants, however, are not bound by the rule against revealing "privileged" client information.

Unless there are unusual complications, you may be better off going it alone with the IRS. You are always your best advocate. You know your circumstances, and only you can find more receipts and substantiations after the audit has begun. A careless tax professional representing you may simply look in the file and say "No, we have no receipts," thus losing you a point that will cost you money. Going it alone gives you more possibilities, more time, and more maneuverability in this nasty game.

Bide your time, look for any possible delay, be composed, and when you need time to produce a record—ask for it. The IRS cannot deny you the right to have ample time to present your case in the best possible way. As you go along, you can always consult with a tax professional on the more difficult issues, without giving up control of your case to someone else. Only you can do this best—if you don't panic.

CHAPTER 9

DAMAGE CONTROL

So you didn't panic, you took your time to answer the letter, and you came to your meeting with the agent. What next? The amount of hassle and damage you receive in the audit depends on many factors—but the most important one is you. At least one person committed suicide following an endless audit. He simply couldn't take the harassment any longer. His son, who was supposed to receive a small refund from the IRS, got a letter from the agency instead, telling him that his refund was applied toward paying some of the tax owed by his deceased father! The truth is that even death will not end your audit. If you die, your executors will have to continue with the audit. You need to remember, however, that you are dealing with a huge and inefficient bureaucracy.

Some people have found that moving to another state, or telling the IRS they will be overseas for a period of time after the IRS requests the audit, has gotten them off the hook. When files are transferred to another location, or when delays are forced on the Service, files may fall through the cracks and the target of the audit goes free.

If this does not happen to you, tough it out. Taking a tough, if civil and polite stance against the IRS is probably your best defense. Asking questions may help dif-

SOMETIMES, IF YOU MOVE TO ANOTHER STATE OR GO OVERSEAS FOR A WHILE AND INFORM THE IRS, THEY WILL DROP YOUR AUDIT

ANYTHING UNUSUAL THAT MAY HAPPEN WITH YOUR FILE COULD GET YOU OFF

fuse the attack against you as well. Try to find out from the agent anything you can about your case. Why is your return being examined? Once you find out—if you do— try to limit the agent's investigation to only that item. Be pushy: If this item is under question, here is the proof you need, now let's get it over with! Of course, this approach may not always work, but it is definitely worth a try. Remember that whatever got your file questioned is only the hook to get someone who looks—statistically—like a person who may lead the government to more money: hidden income treasures, overinflated deductions, who knows....

DO EVERYTHING YOU CAN TO LIMIT THE SCOPE OF THE AUDIT

The IRS agent may want to continue looking at other categories which may lead to the treasures. Effective damage control will be your ability to limit the investigation as much as possible. What may work in your favor, as in any conflict situation, are the weaknesses of your adversary. Agents are overworked, pressed for time, limited in their ability, and often lazy. One trick that often works is to do the agent's homework for him or her. For example, suppose that you forgot a small item you should have declared on your return—an IRA you cashed without reporting and paying the penalty. Do the homework for the agent, do the correction in perfect accounting form, admit the small additional amount you owe and ask the agent to conclude the audit. This face-saving item you gave the auditor, resulting in a small gain for the government, may lead to the case being closed (and possibly costing you much less than if a more thorough investigation were to ensue). You should never, however, concede large items. The agent may never find them; the investigation may lead in other directions, away from the large errors.

IRS agents have access to an incredible array of information about you. Some of the information may be obtained directly from you, other facts from different sources. It is hard to describe just how much someone can learn about you by looking at your canceled checks: virtually everything about your life is there. In an audit, your boxes of canceled checks—copies of which the IRS can get from your financial institutions if you can't find all the checks—may be carefully scrutinized. This doesn't happen in every audit, but it happens whenever the agent decides that an in-depth examination is warranted or when there is a suspicion of hidden income.

Not only will the amounts of your checks be totalled and compared with the deposits to look directly for hidden income, but the names of payees will be scrutinized. The agent will also look for any signs of alteration. Look at your own checks now and ask yourself: Is there anything here that could arouse an auditor's suspicion? Any transfer of funds, and especially foreign exchange, will get you very close attention. In looking for hidden income, the agent can speak to other people who may have knowledge of your lifestyle, as well as obtain other documents directly from you. If you keep a foreign bank account, indirect methods such as looking at your passport can be used by the IRS to determine frequent trips

NEVER BRING TO THE AUDIT ANYTHING OTHER THAN THE ITEMS ASKED FOR

YOUR CANCELED CHECKS TELL THE IRS THE STORY OF YOUR LIFE

to offshore destinations known to have non-reporting foreign banks. Then a more direct inquiry can nail the actual bank account with your hidden income.

Large cash transactions can also tip off the agent. The IRS is well aware that cash, because it is liquid and generally non-traceable, is a good way to hide your transactions. This is one reason why institutions are required to report to the government all cash transactions of $10,000 or more. If you make purchases or transfers of large amounts, records of these transactions may be obtained by the IRS. The agent is then well on the way to finding hidden income.

The IRS has incredible computer power for searching for information on the taxpayer. A computer information system called TECS (Treasury Enforcement Communication System) is a major tool that can be tapped by an agent looking for information on you. Any information the Department of the Treasury may have collected on a taxpayer is coded in TECS. This includes information from the Customs Service on any expensive goods imported from abroad, and any other information Treasury may collect.

A VAST
COMPUTER
NETWORK IS AT
THE DISPOSAL
OF THE IRS IN
ITS SEARCH

Recently, IRS personnel started downloading computer files from a wide variety of sources to workstations and personal computers, where segments of the databases may be analyzed separately in search of information on hidden income sources. The databases used are lists of business transactions of all kinds, memberships in organizations, subscriptions of all kinds, deeds and real estate records, licensing data and more. This approach uses what might be called the chain-letter principle and is similar to the system that gets your name on increasing numbers of mailing lists against your will and without your knowledge. Powerful computers search for your name and social security number in an expanding number of databases that are available to the IRS.

The twin powers of parallel processing and modern computer network design make the IRS ever more efficient in searching for information on any taxpayer. The tremendous advances taking place in this technology help the IRS invade your privacy. This invasion is bound to get much worse in the near future; the IRS apparently already has plans to look at a variety of computer files that include taxpayer information of a very private nature. This may jeopardize the integrity of such information and may involve violation of taxpayers' constitutional rights of privacy. There have already been cases where taxpayers' confidential information has been compromised by IRS personnel who looked at taxpayer information in IRS files and shared the information with unauthorized persons. Be extremely careful with the information you give the IRS. Never give more than they ask for.

THE INFORMATION SUPERHIGHWAY HELPS THE IRS

CHAPTER 10

THE LET'S-MAKE-A-DEAL TRAP

Without looking at all your records and receipts, the agent might suddenly say: "I'll accept half your deductions." This is not a casual remark. It is the result of intensive training the IRS gives its agents. It is part of a new effort the IRS is making in reducing the effort that goes into tax investigations; it wants maximum revenue at minimum cost. Often, when the assessment of additional tax is made and a taxpayer appeals or goes to court, half the new assessments are thrown out. The new approach, which allows half of everything right away, may minimize the effort on the part of the government. The IRS hates appeals, and more than anything, it hates going to court. If you will agree to a fifty-fifty settlement right away, the agency can avoid a lot of trouble.

This approach by the IRS, however, is a trap. First, it assumes that you lied about everything. And now the IRS will do you the favor of "forgiving" half your debt. Even if you really lied, this deal is no bed of roses. If you accept this gambit, you may not gain anything. Yes, the IRS will accept half your claims and make you pay for the other half. But, and here comes the big "but"—first of all, you will have to pay penalties and interest, and these alone may get you closer to the half you thought you were getting away with. Secondly, an important

BEWARE OF AN OFFER BY THE AGENT TO ACCEPT HALF YOUR CLAIMS WITHOUT LOOKING AT ANYTHING

point indeed: the IRS now has you caught. You have just admitted—indirectly—that you lied about your return, and they will get you many, many ways. Your DIF score will rise dramatically, meaning that in the future you will be audited again and again.

SETTLING FOR LESS THAN YOU DESERVE MAY ALSO CONDEMN YOU TO FUTURE AUDITS

As we will discuss next, the audit is not over when one year's return has been examined. The IRS can now look at more years, come back later and audit other years. You will never get out of the hole once you take this bait. Even if you lied about everything, you should never accept a fifty-fifty offer from the IRS. Let them look at every item, while you fight them for it. Give them a run for their money. Make it difficult and lengthy and costly for them to get anything from you. You gain nothing by accepting such an offer.

The worst of it is, of course, when the taxpayer is honest, pays the government what's owed and then gets caught in an audit because, statistically, people in his or her category tend to be picked up by the DIF. Here is a person with legitimate claims and deductions, with receipts for everything, but with limited time to go through an all-consuming audit that can drag on for months and wear out even the toughest among us. The IRS, experts in terrorizing and intimidating, make you this tempting offer. Just say no! Let the IRS agent sweat it out. Fight him or her on every single point. Later, when the tax examination is over, may be the time to make deals. Make deals when you are ahead. Why? Once the examination is over, the IRS agent will make an assessment, to include all the new taxes the agent believes you owe because you lacked substantiation for deductions you claimed. And unreported income will also be added into the assessment if the agent believes there is sufficient evidence. You will now have the choice of either agreeing with the assessment and paying the additional tax and penalties and interest, or appealing to a higher level. It is almost never a good idea to agree. You should always appeal, unless the result of the audit is so much in your favor that there is nothing to appeal—you are getting money back.

Once you inform the agent of your intention to appeal the assessment, the agent will have a strong incentive to make a deal with you, a deal that will be much more in your favor than the deal offered initially. The deal may be on your terms for the simple reason that no IRS agent wants to have his or her work appealed, gone over by a supervisor, scrutinized, and criticized by a higher-ranking IRS official. An appeal makes the agent seem weak and ineffective. At this point, if the agent sees that you intend to appeal, a favorable offer may be made to you. Think about it. You may still want to appeal. And the offers can get better and better as time goes on. If you appeal and lose, and if your case is strong enough, you still retain the option of going to tax court. Tax court usually doesn't require an attorney, unless your case is complicated or the amounts large. Tax court is designed as a People's Court. You present your case and so does the Service, and the judge will make a decision. Going to

DON'T LET THE AGENT PUSH YOU TO SETTLE, GIVING UP YOUR RIGHT TO AN APPEAL

court, however, is costly to the government. If you show you intend to go to court, a more favorable offer to settle out of court may be made to you.

CHAPTER 11

THE HUNT FOR
HIDDEN TREASURE

Your first meeting with the IRS agent is an important
one. Remember that you don't want to give the
agent any information. Information, however, is con-
veyed also by indirect means. IRS agents are trained at
making judgements about your likely actual income
based on your lifestyle. They scrutinize how you look: do
you wear expensive clothing or jewelry, implying a higher standard of living than your reported income would
allow? Do you drive a more expensive car than your
reported income could support? Leave your Porsche at
home...preferably take public transportation to the interview. An IRS interview is one place you don't want to
impress anyone with how much money you have. When
making small talk with the agent, talk about the weather.
Don't talk about your experience cruising the Caribbean,
and it's probably not a good idea to discuss politics.
About the last thing an IRS agent wants to hear from you
is complaints about how your tax dollars are spent.

The treasure-hunting accounting principle:

INCOME = EXPENDITURES + SAVINGS

Or, in simple English: What goes in must come out. The
IRS agent will try to balance your books to his or her sat-

**NEVER
GIVE THE IRS
AGENT THE
IMPRESSION
THAT YOU
HAVE MONEY**

isfaction. The theory is that once everything that goes in has been identified, and everything that comes out has been accounted for as well, the true level of your income will magically emerge.

This approach is at best naive. To see that, just ask yourself if you could do such a balancing act with your own bank books. Once you have been caught in the IRS audit net, the agent will likely ask to see your bank statements and try to match all deposit amounts with all checks written. Look back at your bank books now and see whether you can match the amounts. If you are like most people, you don't have a record of every check written years ago. And what was that $1,500 deposit? You can't remember now. What you cannot remember, the agent will write down as "unsubstantiated" and will assume explicitly was income. Remember that the burden of proof in an audit is on you and not on the IRS—here, you are assumed guilty until you prove your innocence. Try to find—before any audit—a substantiation for every possible item: deposit, check, expense, credit-card charge. Leave nothing to chance or the enemy will use it to hang you.

Another favorite method of the IRS in finding unreported income is the Net Worth method. Here, the auditor computes what he or she believes is your net worth in the beginning of the year and at the end of the year. Your net worth is the sum of the values of all your assets, including all amounts in cash at banks and other financial institutions, minus all your liabilities (your debts, including your mortgage and other loans). Any increase in your net worth over the year will then be checked. If the total increase in your net worth cannot be explained by your reported income as well as other reported sources such as capital gains, gain in property value, the remainder will be attributed to unreported income. This is an indirect method of looking for unreported income. The balance-your-books method is direct because it looks at every visible transaction: deposits, checks, etc. The Net Worth method looks for the total accumulation in the entire year. This method, too, has pitfalls and ample opportunity for errors and abuse by the IRS. As part of this tack of the investigation, the auditor may ask you to fill out Form 4822, listing your living expenses for the year. Most people grossly underestimate their living expenses. Underestimating your living expenses will overestimate the amount remaining and that, in turn, will be interpreted as the result of hidden income!

What makes the search for hidden treasures so preposterous is that people who truly hide income are immune to this kind of matching search. The innocent and the careless are the ones who have unexplained items when the books are balanced in the hands of the IRS. That $1,500 was probably a birthday gift from your mother, or a reimbursed business expense, or maybe you deposited traveler's checks left over from the previous summer's trip to Europe. Truly hidden income would never be casually deposited in a bank, where it can be traced so easily. But try to argue that with the IRS. And

NEVER AGREE TO GIVE THE AUDITOR A LISTING OF YOUR LIVING EXPENSES

the amounts can grow extremely fast. A few items such as these on the deposit side and a few missing checks on the outlay side and the agent will conclude that you had $20,000 in additional, unreported income.

That person who does have $20,000 in unreported income very likely laughs at the silly IRS accountants—his or her books will very neatly balance at the lower, reported amount of income claimed on the tax return. The unreported income most probably was in cash, and it did not go into any bank account; neither did it go toward the purchase of a large item that can be traced and will show an increase in net worth. And if it did, it wasn't a bank account or a property in this country, so it wasn't declared anywhere or reported to the IRS. Hiding income can be relatively easy for the person who realizes that the IRS looks for such income by balancing the visible "in" with the visible "out," or by looking for an increase in visible wealth. The honest person needs to protect him- or herself from false accusations of hidden income.

It is worth noting that many credit card companies now allow their customers to write checks against their credit account, and the amounts are then billed on the customer's usual monthly statement. Such charges, payable to any third party exactly like bank checks, are—at this writing—not reported as bank transactions. You are not sent the canceled check, nor does your statement show who was paid, or a check number. Such transfers of funds may not be visible to the IRS agent conducting an audit.

Again, be careful with the impression you give of yourself to the Service, and understand that there is more to the process than simple book balancing. If your records show large amounts expended on luxury items that the agent suspects are above your means, this could lead to much closer scrutiny even if your books balance. The last thing you want to do is to arouse suspicion. Remember that the IRS has virtually unlimited powers against you. If the agent suspects you of having a larger income to support the expenses he or she believes that you have, the investigation could expand, and you will be faced with having to prove a lot more. You want to be cautious and anticipate problems before you are faced with an audit. Write down a short explanation next to every large or unusual bank deposit or check written. Do your best to appear to live a notch lower than your actual standard of living. This way you will be sure to remain beyond suspicion of having unreported income.

CHAPTER 12

THE MULTI-YEAR CANCER

An IRS audit is a cancer. Like all malignant tumors, it starts small. A little letter, somewhat individualized by handwriting, asking for specific items to be examined. Once you contract the disease, it spreads and spreads. It starts with one year, then the agent asks to see the returns of other years. What most people do not realize about the IRS is that an audit is rarely for one particular tax year only. The initial year is audited because the computer decided that you look like the people who owe more tax. Then, goes IRS logic, if this person owes more tax (even before this assessment is made!), let's see what we can get for other tax years as well. It is important to understand that any tax year may be audited as long as three years have not elapsed since the tax return was filed for that year.

Laws are somewhat ambiguous about when an additional year may be audited, and therefore, the IRS agent will typically be sneaky. But make no mistake, the agent's supervisor strongly encourages the agent to audit other tax years as well as the one currently being examined. Often, the agent will say, while auditing your 1994 return: "Have you filed for 1995 yet? I would like to look at your file to see how you handled this item in

1995, for comparison." If you give the agent your 1995 return, you have just helped the agent start another audit!

The best technique, as always, is to delay. Tell the agent you will "look for it at home," and then say nothing about it the next time you meet with him or her. Hopefully, the investigator, overworked and eager to finish, will forget or give up on it. Legally, you may ignore such requests as long as they are not in writing. If the IRS agent requests in writing to see other years, you must submit the returns. Which years may be audited by the IRS?

THE IRS WILL TRY TO EXPAND THE AUDIT TO INCLUDE AS MANY OTHER TAX YEARS AS POSSIBLE

Any tax return that has been filed by the time of the audit and for which the three-year time limit on audits has not yet expired is called an "open" year. The IRS has the right to audit any open year. For example, suppose that you always file your return on April 15th, when it is due. On April 15th of 1993 you filed your 1992 tax return; on April 15, 1994, you filed for 1993; and on April 15, 1995 you filed your 1994 return. Now suppose that in March 1996 you are audited for tax year 1993. Since three years have not yet elapsed since April 1993, tax year 1992 is still open. The agent can therefore also audit your 1992 return. The year 1991 is no longer open since the time limit for that tax year was exceeded on April 15, 1995. Now comes a very important point. If your audit continues past April 15th of 1996, what should you do? Do not file your 1995 return! If you do file, the IRS agent can now audit that year as well—as it will have just become "open." Ask for an automatic extension to file your tax return late (by August 15). If your audit is still not over by early August, ask for a second extension, which the IRS will grant if you have a good reason, allowing you to file by October 15. With luck, your case will then be over.

The wisdom of this advice has even been admitted by an IRS agent who said to me: "Don't tell my boss I told you this, but no one should ever file while being audited." While you are under audit, the IRS agent will bring up your record on the computer. The computer is programmed to show all open years. The built-in calendar adjusts to show which years have been filed, which can no longer be audited, and which are currently open, making it easy for the IRS to conduct audits of all allowable years. Auditing more years for a person suspected initially of hiding income or over-claiming deductions can be a profitable undertaking for the government. No new resources are required, as an agent already working on the taxpayer's audit conducts the subsequent investigations. And such expanded audits have a good chance for added revenue.

Of course this system is absurd, as it can result in an "endless" audit for the unlucky person caught in this web. If you do file your returns when they are due while an audit is in progress—for example, you file for 1995 on April 15, 1996, while your audits for 1993 and 1994 are in progress—the agent can now audit also 1995. This year will appear on the computer screen as soon as the

**NEVER FILE
A TAX RETURN
WHILE AN AUDIT IS
IN PROGRESS**

**USE ANY EXCUSE
YOU CAN TO KEEP
THE AGENT AWAY
FROM YOUR OTHER
OPEN YEARS**

IRS gets your file. Now the IRS has until April 15, 1999, to complete the audit for the 1995 tax year. The next April 15, assuming the audit is still in progress—and it often is—the IRS can start auditing the 1996 return, and so on ad infinitum. Sadly, there is absolutely nothing you can do if the IRS wants to continue auditing you forever, year after year. The limitations are exceeded one year at a time, and if you do not give them an extension to finish their work for each year, they will simply close the year when it is due, and go on to auditing the next year. Usually the audit does not go on forever, but long audits, covering four or more tax years, are not uncommon. The Service strongly encourages this practice. Do not confuse this with the limitation on the IRS not to audit the same item on a third year if the item was audited on either of the previous two years and no additional tax was due. This stipulation of the tax code is often circumvented in the open years approach, first, because the audits are done at the same time (these aren't new audits generated by the computer, but rather a continuation to other years of a single, initial audit), and second, because it is easy for the IRS to find additional tax for at least some item in a given year, and then go on to other years.

Admittedly, not filing a return while an audit is in progress may not always help you, especially if the IRS is really out to get you, since eventually the extensions you request will expire and you will have to file. If an audit truly drags on, this may happen. However, remember that you are dealing with an extremely inefficient bureaucracy. Usually, buying more time will improve your position, and in most cases an extension will carry you to the end of the audit without submitting yet another open year to the audit cancer.

CHAPTER 13

THE COHAN RULE, AND: WHAT'S REASONABLE?

When the IRS agent audits your expenses to verify the validity of the deductions you claimed on your return, he or she looks for receipts to substantiate every item. For every expense you incurred, you are expected to provide a written receipt. You are also expected to substantiate your reason for claiming the item. Was the payment you made necessary for conducting your business? When a claim cannot be substantiated by showing a receipt, or when the reason for the expense is not accepted, the agent will disallow the claimed item, concluding that either you did not incur the expense, or it wasn't necessary for your business or employment. When everything is totalled, you may realize that you have lost a significant portion of the deductions you used to offset your tax bill. Then interest is added, and penalties. You are being punished for making false claims to the IRS.

To the auditor, a claim without an actual receipt is a false claim. However, in 1930, the entertainer George M. Cohan ("I'm a Yankee Doodle Dandy") went to court against the IRS. Cohan did not have receipts for all of his business expenses. The court took the position that even if records are not complete, the IRS should

IN LOOKING AT YOUR DEDUCTIONS THE IRS AGENT HAS ONE OBJECTIVE: TO DISALLOW

THE COHAN RULE
SAYS YOU
MAY BE ABLE TO
CLAIM SOME
DEDUCTIONS WITH-
OUT ACTUAL
RECEIPTS IF
THEY SEEM
REASONABLE
(BUT IT'S HIGHLY
ADVISABLE TO
HAVE RECEIPTS
FOR EVERYTHING)

allow such expenses if they are reasonable. The court's ruling that lack of evidence does not automatically take away your right to deductions became a landmark decision. So if you can justify your expenses and they seem reasonable given your occupation, the IRS may accept some of these deductions if pushed to do so. If you have to go to court, the court may allow an estimated value for some deductions without receipts, although these amounts will be less than the full amount you failed to prove with receipts. The Cohan rule, however, does not apply to travel and entertainment expenses, as these were viewed as easily abused for personal rather than business purposes.

It is still always the best policy to keep perfect receipts if at all possible. It is also a very good idea to keep a journal of all of your expenses as back-up and reinforcement for the receipts you have. If the IRS disputes some of your items, you may mention to the agent the Cohan rule, and there may be a sudden change in attitude as the agent realizes that you know the law and are willing to fight.

KEEP A JOURNAL
DESCRIBING ALL
YOUR BUSINESS
EXPENSES TO BACK
YOUR RECEIPTS
AND OTHER
SUBSTANTIATION

Beyond keeping receipts and journals to substantiate your deductions, remember that you will also have to prove to the IRS that your deductions are indeed justified for conducting your business. This accountant's mindset, even more than receipts and other substantiation, is a key to winning your audit. Your adversary is much more crafty and cynical when it comes to trying to take away your right to claim deductions than they are in questioning your receipts. In finding a way to disallow your expenses, the IRS has a formidable legal tool in its arsenal:

The IRS follows some definite guidelines that it has set up in determining what is reasonable in any given category. If your deductions in a given area exceed these guidelines, the IRS will decide that your entire category of deductions should be disallowed. If you are a farmer, and you incur high expenses in running your farm, the IRS may decide that you are a Gentleman (Gentlewoman) Farmer and disallow all deductions for farm expenses. This is an incredibly powerful tool. Make sure you can prove that your business is not a hobby. The IRS has a "3-out-of-5" rule for throwing out your business deductions: If in at least three out of five years your business has not shown a profit, it can be determined a hobby. While this rule is not cast in stone, the IRS requires the taxpayer to prove the legitimacy of a business. The key here is to demonstrate to the IRS that you are trying to make a profit—and not just using the business as a tax writeoff. In an audit of such items, the agent will look at other years as well, giving the IRS an excuse to examine other open years, and setting new traps for you. The same consideration will be used in capitalization issues, for example, writing off the cost of a computer you bought one year over its expected life of several years. You should be aware of all these issues when preparing your taxes, realizing that these issues may come back to haunt you in an audit.

THE IRS CAN DECIDE THAT YOUR BUSINESS IS A HOBBY AND FLATLY DISALLOW ALL YOUR BUSINESS DEDUCTIONS

CHAPTER 14

APPEAL

Once the audit process is over, the IRS agent issues a report with any adjustments to your tax bill based on the audit. If you disagree with the agent's findings, you have several options. It is highly recommended that you pursue at least some of these options. It is very rarely in your best interest to agree with the IRS.

After looking at the examination report, call the agent and explain why you disagree with the findings. There is a chance that the agent will compromise with you and reduce the amount of added tax demanded. If not, ask to meet with the agent's supervisor. An IRS group manager will usually support the findings of the auditor—but not always. You now have a new chance to explain your case to the manager and, using the techniques described earlier, this time you may be successful.

The group manager has an incentive to come to your side. The reason is, as usual, statistics. The auditor's performance is judged by the IRS based on the number of cases closed with the taxpayer's agreement. The government spends money and time when the taxpayer does not agree with the agent's report and appeals. Therefore, not only the agent, but also the supervisor, look better if your case can be settled without appeal. If you calmly explain your reasons, there is a chance they will come

IT IS ALWAYS A GOOD IDEA TO TRY TO MEET THE AGENT'S SUPERVISOR

toward you. If not, you still haven't lost anything. If you are not satisfied, launch an official appeal to the IRS. The IRS has an administrative procedure for appealing examination results. The appeal process is simple and does not cost you anything, and it is likely that your tax bill will be reduced. It is true that the appeals officer can legally review your entire file and that this process may actually increase the amount you owe. The IRS likes to tell you this to reduce the likelihood that you'll take advantage of your right to appeal. Practically speaking, however, an expanded examination is rare, so usually the appeal will reduce your bill. There is another important reason for appealing: time. The appeals process extends the time involved, and remember that time always works in your favor—anything can still go wrong and you may have to pay nothing. According to IRS statistics, appeals result in an average reduction of your tax bill by over 40 percent!

Clearly, the IRS does not want you to appeal. The Service has forms for every possible purpose, except for appeals! So you need to write your own protest letter to the IRS District Director in order to request an appeal of your audit results. You should do so immediately after receiving the letter notifying you of the examination report and the proposed adjustments to your tax bill. This official notification, called the "30 Day Letter," carries with it the right to appeal, but the appeal must be requested within the 30-day time limit. In your letter, explain why you disagree with the audit results and include copies of the 30-day letter and the examination report. You do not have to show that the examination results are completely false, but rather that you have an arguable position in disputing the auditor's findings. You will have several months to prepare your appeal; use your time wisely. Review everything presented at the audit, and look for additional information. New information, if you can find it, may make a big difference in the outcome of the appeal. Try to find new and better ways to present your case—try to provide better documentation for your deductions and claims. Think of better explanations that you can make in trying to convince the appeals officer that you are right. It may be a good idea to bring witnesses to corroborate your claims.

The appeals officer who will hear your case is probably older and more experienced than the auditor, and has more latitude in deciding your case. The appeals officer is judged by how many cases he or she settles with the taxpayer, rather than on backing up the original auditor's report. If you want to make a deal with the IRS, now may be the time to do so to your advantage, especially if you have some new documentation. The appeals officer makes a serious assessment of the risk of litigation. The officer will weigh your perceived determination to go to court should the appeal not end in your favor, and will also assess the government's chance of winning its case in court.

In recent years, most of the resources of the IRS have been allocated to computerization and other mod-

IT USUALLY PAYS (OFTEN QUITE WELL) TO APPEAL

ernization efforts rather than to increase the ranks of IRS attorneys ready to do battle in tax court. Since legal resources are scarce, the IRS tries—whenever possible—to avoid going to court with you. In your appeal, you must demonstrate to the appeals officer that you have a chance of winning the case if it goes to tax court.

THE IRS DOES NOT WANT YOU TO GO TO COURT—USE THIS FACT TO YOUR ADVANTAGE

Start preparing for a possible court case by conducting preliminary legal research of the issues involved. Look for precedents or legal rulings in cases that are similar to yours so you can see what the courts' decisions have been on the issues at stake. The fact that you are well-prepared to go to court may convince the appeals officer to negotiate a compromise decision in your case. Over 85% of all appeals are settled without going to court. However, if you fail in your appeal, you should definitely consider going to tax court.

In small cases (less than $10,000 in dispute for any one year), no attorney is necessary. The tax court in such cases works like small claims court. You present your case informally and the judge makes a decision. The tax court is independent of the IRS, and it offers you yet another chance of presenting your case and beating the results of the audit. Going to court will, again, buy you more time—filing a petition to go to court will get you a year or more before the tax bill is due. Remember that interest continues to run on the amount you ultimately owe. However, you can stop the interest clock from ticking by paying the IRS the amount they claim is due, and later receiving a full or partial refund if you win your case.

Most often, the IRS is not certain to win its case against you, so going to court will give you yet another opportunity to settle the case without a trial. In fact, over 85% of the cases that are filed against the IRS are settled without a trial. Going to court is not likely to bring you a complete victory; however, about half the cases that do go to court bring at least some reduction of your original bill.

Filing a Tax Court Petition without valid grounds can get you in trouble, as such cases are considered frivolous. Going to court without justification can result in a fine of up to $5,000. If you do have a good case, by all means file a petition. After you file, you will hear from the IRS attorney handling the case, giving you yet another chance to settle your case without an actual trial. You can settle the case with the IRS attorney at any time as long as the judge has not made a ruling.

If you do go to trial, prepare your case well before your day in court. Bring documents and witnesses if you can. Make your presentation short and to the point. Consider giving the judge a written outline of your arguments demonstrating why you believe you do not owe the tax. The judge's decision will be made known to you in about a month or so, and that decision is final, without possibility of further appeal. The ruling is usually brief, listing the amount of tax and any penalties that may apply.

What we described above applies to the Tax Court Small Claims Procedure. If your case is not small, you need an attorney. There are also other courts where your case against the IRS may be heard. You can pay the amount the IRS says you owe and then sue for a refund in a Federal District Court or in the Claims Court in Washington, D.C. In both places you will need an attorney.

CHAPTER 15

THE TAX COLLECTOR

Once appeals are exhausted, you are faced with having to pay. The collection division of the IRS is a hungry beast. Whenever the IRS determines that you owe more money, you will get a first request to pay the determined amount. If payment is not received in 30 to 60 days, the IRS issues a series of reminders over several weeks. If all of these are ignored, the IRS then sends you a final notice, after which it can start enforced collection of the tax. Levy (seizure) orders can now be issued to third parties that have money belonging to you—employers and banks where you have accounts. If you cannot pay, you should respond in writing to the requests. If you ask specifically for 60 days to make payment (the maximum allowed), and include a small payment with your request to show your intention to pay, you can buy more time. Often this may delay the hungry shark from coming after you by as much as several months or more.

If you fail to pay the Service Center, which issues the notices, your file will be transferred to the IRS's Automated Collection System (ACS). This is a computer system designed to collect the tax. The ACS is a sinister resident of cyberspace. It is a sophisticated computing network designed to collect information about you from

THE TAX COLLECTOR HAS AN IMPRESSIVE ARRAY OF WEAPONS AT HIS OR HER DISPOSAL

as many sources as possible: state and local agencies such as motor vehicle departments, and other licensing offices, as well as banks and registries of all kinds. The ACS is the machinery that locates any asset you own or money you hold that can then be fed to the shark. As soon as the ACS locates a levy source, it sends a notice to seize. It is impossible for a taxpayer to deal with this vicious, impersonal computer system. The best you can do is to try to have the IRS District Office get back your file from the ACS so you can negotiate a payment plan with them, buy more time, and have the seizure stopped. It is very difficult to stop a levy against your bank accounts.

Once property you own has been seized, you may still redeem it from the IRS if you can make payment of the tax demanded and the expenses incurred in seizing the property. You may also convince the IRS to release the levy if you can show your intent to pay.

JEOPARDY ASSESSMENT

A jeopardy assessment is probably the most powerful collection tool of the IRS, and the one most open to abuse of the taxpayer.

A JEOPARDY
ASSESSMENT
CAN BE MADE
WITHOUT PRIOR
NOTICE TO THE
TAXPAYER

When the IRS makes a jeopardy assessment against you, the rules of the game are abandoned. The IRS does not grant you even the courtesy of a notice. A jeopardy assessment allows the IRS to demand immediately full payment of the amount it claims is due, or require the posting of a bond for this full amount. The amount of a jeopardy assessment is almost always larger than the actual tax liability. If the taxpayer does not pay, the IRS can seize money, property, or other assets, before the taxpayer has the chance to respond. It is, of course, sheer abuse of power. One expects such things in countries where human rights are violated, but make no mistake about it—the government of the United States of America can take away your property without notice, without explanation, and without leaving you any recourse.

The IRS may invoke a jeopardy assessment against you any time it believes that tax collection will be jeopardized by delay. If you are audited by the IRS and the agent conducting the investigation becomes suspicious that in case additional tax is assessed against you, you will flee the country, a jeopardy assessment may be made. Auditors will sometimes abuse their power and threaten a taxpayer that if he or she does not cooperate a jeopardy assessment will be made. Sometimes the agent will be bluffing, other times he or she may actually mean it. The potential abuse of power is virtually limitless.

Legally, the IRS can invoke a jeopardy assessment if it suspects one of the following:

1. The taxpayer is preparing to leave the country, or
2. The taxpayer plans to transfer his or her assets to a destination outside the country where the IRS may not be able to seize it, or
3. The taxpayer is preparing to hide assets, spend his or her money, or transfer monies and property to others, or
4. The taxpayer may become financially insolvent.

An IRS examiner does not have the authority to order a jeopardy assessment, but a regional or a district director of the IRS has this power. The agent must send a recommendation for the jeopardy assessment to the higher-ups in the IRS bureaucracy, who can then make the assessment. A jeopardy assessment short-circuits any judicial review of the position of the IRS in the audit by allowing the assessment to be made without first sending the taxpayer a notice of deficiency.

At times, IRS agents will threaten a taxpayer with a jeopardy assessment if the taxpayer refuses to sign the form allowing the IRS to extend its investigation beyond the usual three-year limit. The IRS says that if you don't sign away your rights they will take away even more of your rights—in fact, strip you of virtually all your rights to due process. While it is questionable whether the IRS can legally do this, there have been some old cases where a jeopardy assessment was made in such circumstances. Schnepper (1978, p. 2) recounts a number of horror stories where the IRS' power to issue a jeopardy assessment was abused. One of them is about a major in the United States Army whose wife needed a life-saving operation. Four months before any tax was due, the major wrote to the IRS, explaining that he worried about not having enough money to pay his taxes because of his wife's operation, and requesting a meeting with an IRS agent to arrange a way for him to pay off his taxes for the year. The IRS swiftly responded to the letter with a "jeopardy and termination assessment," freezing the major's bank account just when he needed the money for his wife's operation. Burnham (1989, p. 64) tells the bizarre story of Sharon Willits, who was investigated by the IRS in 1973. When it was determined that Ms. Willits had not filed a tax return in four years, the IRS arbitrarily decided that her annual income was $60,000, and issued a jeopardy assessment against her assets in the amount of $25,000. On appeal, it was determined that Ms. Willits was actually living on monthly alimony payments of $135 and the $2,000 proceeds from the sale of the house she had won as part of her divorce settlement. The Court of Appeals further concluded that the IRS' seizure of Ms. Willits' property was based on a purely fictitious income assessment.

CHAPTER 16

AVOIDING AN AUDIT:
AN OVERVIEW

Now that you've seen how bad things can get for you once you are the subject of an audit, and after considering ways to fight back, it's time to begin our discussion of ways to avoid the ordeal altogether—how to minimize your taxes while also minimizing the chance of an audit. In short, how to beat the IRS at its own game!

Remember that the information on your tax return is entered into the IRS computer by keypunch operators who are hired part-time, poorly trained, and pushed by their supervisors to enter the data quickly. Your return is keypunched in an extremely short time. It stands to reason that the number of numerical elements from each return entered into the computer to be analyzed by the DIF—the Discriminant Function procedure used by the IRS to determine who should be audited—is not very large (although the IRS would have you think the DIF is very complicated...). My own analysis of a sample of 1,289 audited and unaudited returns in chase of the DIF indeed confirms this hypothesis. In fact, my extensive computer analyses on a Cray-2 supercomputer revealed that a handful of variables account for about 90% of all audits. We will concentrate on understanding these variables in the following chapters, and on showing how these variables should be measured and manipulated to reduce the chance of an audit to a minimum.

What about the remaining 10%? These audits are caused by factors extraneous to the actual DIF analysis done by the IRS. Mathematical errors caught by the computer will trigger a mail audit that may expand to a full-scale audit (but may also prevent one). Previous audits raise the DIF and can cause new audits. Then there is the relatively small probability that the return will be chosen purely at random for a TCMP audit. Certain professions are likely to be audited because from time to time the IRS makes policy decisions to look more carefully at one industry or another. Also, any inconsistencies on your tax return will raise the chance of an audit. These include disagreement of what you report on your federal tax return with what you report on your state tax return; wrong names or other information about your dependents; inconsistencies in information from year to year, and other factors. All of these comprise a fraction of all audits. While arithmetical errors can be avoided, as can the "nice-numbers" trap, one can hardly help belonging to a particular profession or having been audited in the past. We will therefore concentrate on avoiding the factors that cause the majority, 90%, of audits.

Things To Avoid and To Check for in your Return:

1. Nice, whole numbers (such as: $2,000, instead of $1,988.91)
2. Inconsistencies across years (If your daughter changed her name in 1995, let the IRS know about it so they don't audit you, suspecting a fake dependent when comparing your 1994 return with the 1995 return.)
3. Agreement of state return information with that reported on the federal form.
4. Inexplicable large shifts in income and/or expenses from year to year.

The approach we will take is that of quality control. We will carefully construct our tax return, first checking for the minor problems listed above. Then we will look at the variables that cause the majority of the audits and find ways to minimize their impact. These variables are important ratios. These ratios were detected by the computer when I instructed it to try every imaginable combination of variables to find the mix of factors that best explained the difference between returns that are audited and those that are not. This is where an artificial intelligence approach, and a supercomputer, were needed. With 1,289 returns, 631 of which were audited and 658 unaudited, and with a large number of possible combinations to check, it was imperative to find an efficient estimation method. Artificial intelligence is the art of making the computer emulate human thought. To achieve this aim, I used a program that made the computer "think." The computer tried a sequence of variables and looked for the best separation between the two groups of returns. When the best single variable was found, combinations of this variable with all other variables were tested. Then the best combination was checked against combinations with the remaining variables, and so on. At any point in the process, the computer would check the validity of variables chosen earlier in the presence of ones chosen later. If a variable or combination of variables was no longer the best, it was dropped. The result of this exhaustive search was the ratios soon to be discussed.

I will also give some important rules that seem to work very well in general in helping to reduce the chance of an audit—regardless of the factor causing the audit! These are given in the next two chapters. But before we get there I would like to say a few things about two topics on which I am often asked to comment.

Computer Tax-Preparation Programs

The computer programs on the market that help you do your taxes are generally very good. One clear advantage of these programs is that they will print out your 1040 form and associated schedules and forms, thus making your return look professional. Form appearance is very important in working to reduce your audit probability since neat-looking returns convey to the IRS the impression that you know what you are doing. A return that looks good is less likely to be picked for an audit than a sloppily written one. However, don't count on computer tax preparation programs to offer you any serious audit-protection. The program will typically make sure that no math errors exist, and will alert you to what its designers consider to be factors that raise the audit probability. These are very limited and unsophisticated checks that alert you when particular deductions are above the "average" or the "norm." They fall far short of the checks I provide you in this book, which lie close to the frontier between the audit and no-audit groups, rather than a meaningless average for all taxpayers. In short, computer tax-preparation programs are a good tool, but do not rely on them to protect you from an audit or to minimize your tax bill.

Electronic Filing of Tax Returns

The IRS dream, which may soon become a reality, is to have everyone in America file tax returns electronically. And it is easy to see why. If everyone files electronically, returns will be filed early, require far fewer employees to process them, and—most important from an audit point of view—make accessible all the information from tax returns for analysis.

Remember that currently only 40% of the information on a tax return is actually keypunched and input into the IRS computer. Hence, for mailed tax returns, only 40% of the data on the return can be used by the DIF to determine audits. But an electronically filed

**ELECTRONICALLY
FILED RETURNS
GIVE THE IRS MORE
INFORMATION
THAN THE
KEYPUNCHED
RETURNS FILED
BY MAIL.
HOWEVER,
ELECTRONIC
RETURNS ESCAPED
AUDIT RECENTLY
DUE TO A PROBLEM
THE IRS NOW
CLAIMS TO HAVE
SOLVED**

return tells the IRS computer everything. Now, there is an interesting anomaly to consider. While no longer in its infancy, electronic filing is still a relatively new option, and it appears that the large bureaucracy of the IRS still hasn't fully gotten used to it. From published reports as well as tax practitioners' findings it seems that last year the IRS audit machine missed all the electronically filed returns. The IRS promises, however, that this oversight has now been corrected and that electronically filed returns will be subject to audit just like conventionally filed forms. So, the choice is yours at this point, and it is a hard one: believe the IRS that electronic returns will be audited like others and file by mail to avoid giving the IRS more than 40% of your data to work with, or choose not to believe the IRS and take your chances with electronic filing, assuming they still haven't solved the problem and will not audit these returns.

CHAPTER 17

DELAY!

The IRS allows taxpayers to file their income tax returns late. The first such extension is, in fact, automatic! That is, the taxpayer is guaranteed an extension of the time to file the return by filing the appropriate form (FORM 4868) by April 15. This first extension pushes the deadline to file the return from April 15 four months ahead to August 15. Of course, taxes are due on April 15 and must be paid then. You should therefore estimate the tax you owe for the year and send the IRS a check for that amount accompanying the extension request form. Interest will be charged on all late payments. There is also a penalty in case of underpayment of over 10% of the taxbill settled with the extended return.

A second extension of time is possible, but must be approved by the IRS. File Form 2688 with an explanation of the reasons you need the extension. Compelling reasons must be stated for the Service to approve the request. This second extension will further push the time to file two months, to October 15.

Again, remember that the estimated tax, as close to the actual liability as possible, is due April 15.

The data in my study strongly indicate that filing late reduces the chance of an audit, as I will show below. This statistical finding makes a lot of sense.

THE IRS ALLOWS AN AUTOMATIC, NO-QUESTIONS-ASKED EXTENSION TO FILE BY AUGUST 15

A SECOND EXTENSION OF THE TIME TO FILE, WITH REASONS, MAY BE GRANTED, PUSHING THE DEADLINE TO OCTOBER 15

Remember that the IRS game is a timed game, and that time—by the very nature of the audit process—works in your favor.

FILING LATE REDUCES YOUR AUDIT PROBABILITY

Let's look again at the time frame for audits. Most individual taxpayers file their returns by April 15. Five percent of the taxpayers file for the automatic extension, and one percent file for a second extension to October 15. With 95% of the returns keypunched and entered into the system by mid- to late April, the IRS machine—ever pressed for time—is ready to roll. The DIF starts working on the computer records of over 100 million taxpayers right away. Now, the 1995 IRS policy dictates that 2.21 percent of all tax returns be audited (although the percentage will vary from state to state and across national regions). Once the returns that have been identified by the DIF as needing an audit are tagged, there is no time to waste, because of the three-year limit on completing the audits. It stands to reason that late-filed returns may be scrutinized by the DIF after the allotted quota of 2.21 percent nationally has been reached and no audits are to follow. It is even possible that late-filed returns may not be analyzed by the DIF at all. Even if your late-filed return is ultimately pegged for an audit, time is now more likely to run out on the IRS, and this could benefit you. Your audit may even be dropped if unusual further delays or other circumstances intervene.

Unless there are other considerations, such as wanting to get your refund as quickly as possible, you should definitely file for an extension. In addition to the automatic extension, look for any legitimate excuse you can find (although it must be convincing or the IRS will reject it) and request a second extension to October 15. In my study, returns submitted late that otherwise (for the reasons explained in following chapters) should have been audited by the IRS were not audited. This was especially true for returns that were filed after a second extension to October 15. Out of 1,289 returns, 73 were filed late, and of these, not one was audited. This fact, alone, may not mean much since the overall audit probability was then only about one percent. However, twelve of the 73 late-filed returns reported information that—based on the rules explained in the following chapters—would have made them likely to be audited. Seventeen returns had very high ratio-based audit probability. The fact that these returns were not audited certainly suggests that filing late reduces the audit vulnerability. Twelve of the late-filed returns were filed on October 15 (using a second extension) and none were audited. Of these twelve returns, three had extremely high ratio-based audit probabilities. The last return, in fact, violated very strongly two of the ratio-rules I give in the following chapters. I believe that these facts speak for themselves.

Remember that the rules given here and elsewhere in this book are statistical ones. They work in general by reducing the probability of an audit. They do not give you a guarantee that you will not be audited. Since statistics is the name of the game, no one can give you a

FILE THE AUTOMATIC EXTENSION REQUEST AND LOOK FOR ANY LEGITIMATE REASON FOR ASKING FOR A SECOND EXTENSION, TO FILE BY OCTOBER 15 guarantee—the best we can do is to minimize the chance that your return will be audited. New returns I analyzed in 1995, however, all confirmed the rules given here, so I feel confident that you will do well by following the advice.

CHAPTER 18

EXPLAIN

The second general rule that emerged from my analysis of a large number of returns—and even more important than the rule in the previous chapter—is that written explanations go a very long way in reducing your audit probability.

Remember that computers, however useful, do not conduct audits. People are the ones who ultimately decide whether or not to audit you, and it is people who actually conduct the audit. Once the DIF marks you to be audited, your file is picked up by a classifier, an employee of the IRS trained at determining whether or not to take the computer's recommendation to audit you. Until recently, the IRS policy has been to audit only about 10% of the returns tagged by the DIF. But since the audit rate is going up this year, it stands to reason that we may expect a higher number of DIF-tagged returns to be actually audited in the future. At any rate, only some percentage of the DIF-tagged returns are audited, and this means that even if your return looks bad from a statistical point of view, and the computer has indeed identified your return as warranting an audit, your chances of an actual audit are still relatively small. What determines your fate now? The answer lies in how your return looks to the human eye, not the machine.

This means that you should include convincing, valid written explanations for everything you claim on your return. If one of the ratios described in the following chapters goes critical on you and triggers the IRS computer to spit out your return, you want the person looking at your file to say: "AHA! Now I understand why there are all these deductions on Schedule C. This all looks fine to me. Do not audit!" You are also giving the IRS a sample of the defense you are likely to launch in an audit, and since the IRS looks for maximum revenue at minimum effort, they will be more likely to leave you alone. Documentation should anticipate questions the IRS is likely to ask in an audit. If you give them the answers beforehand, why would they audit you?

This point cannot be over-emphasized in this book. You want the IRS people looking at your return to be convinced that you have prepared it correctly, however unusual your circumstances may be from a statistical point of view. If you pass the test of scrutiny by an IRS employee, there will never be an audit.

YOU WANT THE IRS
EMPLOYEE LOOKING
AT YOUR RETURN TO
UNDERSTAND WHY
YOU HAVE
PREPARED IT AS
YOU DID, AND
THEREFORE TO
DECIDE THAT NO
AUDIT IS
NECESSARY

To achieve this goal, you must think about everything while preparing your tax return. Note the reasons for every expense; explain every deduction, loss or contribution. Include explanations that show you are familiar with the tax law pertaining to particular deductions. Then type your explanations neatly on sheets that look professional. Use a computer, if possible. Convince the IRS employee that you have indeed done a thorough job of both calculating your deductions and validating them.

Include your explanation sheets as supplements. An example is shown here.

SUPPLEMENT NO. 1

Job-Related Expenses other than Travel, Meals and Entertainment

A. EDUCATIONAL EXPENSES:

These expenses were incurred as part of my attendance at a seminar on improved direct-marketing methods at the University of California on May 3-18 to learn new techniques necessary for my job as Marketing Director at my company. The seminar was not necessary for meeting minimum requirements for holding my job, nor was it necessary for qualifying for a new job. The seminar improved my job performance.

Tuition at Seminar	$1,560.00
Books	$275.00
Supplies	$105.00
Total:	$1,940.00

B. EQUIPMENT:

1. Home Computer and peripherals: The computer is used 95% for my work: preparing reports, doing budgets, forecasting sales. Purchased 3/17/94.

Purchase price:	$6,125.00
Expensing Deduction:	
95% x 6,125 =	$5,818.75

2. Other equipment purchased in 1994:

Calculator	$ 89.50

Computer software $ 97.25
Total: $186.75

3. Books. These are needed to further my mastery of marketing methods needed for my company to stay competitive in its field.

Twenty eight books were purchased in 1994, names and prices follow. Total cost: $672.13

Returns that look neat, are typed or prepared on a computer and have ample explanations throughout on additional pages will reduce your audit probability. Twenty-two returns in my sample had a high ratio-based audit probability but were not audited; they included neatly-typed, clear explanations as supplements. Six returns in the sample, which had a small ratio-based audit probability were audited, and all of them were sloppily hand-written (possibly, the information on at least some of these returns was incorrectly input into the computer, leading to the audit).

NEAT-LOOKING, COMPUTER-PREPARED RETURNS WITH JUDICIOUS COMMENTS AND EXPLANATIONS ON ATTACHED SHEETS GO A LONG WAY IN CONVINCING THE IRS THAT YOU NEED NOT BE AUDITED

CHAPTER 19

DEVELOPING YOUR PERSONAL ACCOUNTING RATIOS

We now get to the actual variables in the return that trigger the DIF and make the computer decide that you should be audited. All the variables that were picked by my sophisticated statistical and artificial-intelligence algorithms used in analyzing the sample of 1,289 returns (in a way that mimics the DIF used by the IRS) were ratios of amounts that appear in various locations on the tax return. I will now explain how you should compute these ratios while preparing your return, and test them following the rules I give in the following chapter.

We will define a personal accounting ratio (PAR), as the ratio of two quantities that appear on your return. The ratios are numbers that will be decimals between 0 and 1 if the quantity in the numerator is smaller than the quantity in the denominator. If the numerator is greater than the denominator, the ratio will be a number (with decimals) that is greater than 1.00.

MAIN VARIABLES THAT TRIGGER THE DIF ARE RATIOS

PAR for Schedule A

Let us look at the first PAR, the PAR for Schedule A. Look at the bottom of the page on Schedule A. The last line is: "Total Itemized Deductions." Suppose that when you finished preparing your Schedule A, that figure comes out to be $15,000. (Beware! This is used only for demonstration purposes; in reality avoid "nice" numbers.) Now look at the figure you report on line 31 of your 1040 tax form. This is your Adjusted Gross Income (AGI). Suppose that this figure is $60,000. We define the Schedule A PAR as:

PAR(A)=

$$\frac{\text{Total Itemized Deductions on Schedule A}}{\text{Adjusted Gross Income on Form 1040}}$$
$$= \$15,000/\$60,000 = 0.25.$$

Why ratios? When a large number of possible variables were entered into a computer in order to analyze the returns in a way that discriminates between audited and unaudited returns, I discovered that ratios were statistically most significant. This makes a lot of sense because ratios are also percents. To answer the question: "What is reasonable?" it is best to look at ratios. If your income is $60,000 and you have Schedule A deductions of $15,000, then your deductions amount to 25% (the ratio is 0.25) of your income. If, on the other hand, your income was only $20,000 and your Schedule A deductions were, as before, $15,000, then your PAR is 15,000/20,000=0.75, or 75% of your income! The little that is publicly written about the IRS's secret DIF says that it considers different criteria for different income levels. This confirms that ratios are indeed the way to go, as they allow a comparison that accounts for different incomes.

PAR for Schedule C

We define your personal accounting ratio for Schedule C as:

PAR(C)=

$$\frac{\text{Total Expenses on Schedule C (Line 28 + Line 30)}}{\text{Gross Income on Schedule C (Line 7)}}$$

If you don't file a Schedule C, your PAR(C)=0.

Suppose that you had total expenses on Line 28 of Schedule C amounting to $25,000, and that you had additional expenses for business use of your home (Line 30 of Schedule C) amounting to $8,000. Now let's assume that your gross income on Schedule C (Line 7) was $100,000. Then your personal accounting ratio for Schedule C is:

PAR(C)= (25,000 + 8,000)/100,000= 0.33 (or 33%)

What about losses? How are these accounted for by the PAR? The answer is that here is where the PAR exceeds 1.00. Let's look at an example. Suppose your business reported on Schedule C had gross income of $30,000 but your expenses reported on Line 28 were $50,000, and you did not use your home (Line 30 expenses are zero). Your personal accounting ratio for Schedule C is:

PAR(C)=
50,000/30,000= 1.667 (or 166.7%)

It is interesting to note that the IRS's DIF will pick you up for an audit long before you show a loss, as in this example. The trigger points are well below the break-even PAR of 1.00.

PAR for Schedule F

Your personal accounting ratio for Schedule F (assuming you file a Schedule F, otherwise it is defined as zero) is as follows:

PAR(F)=

$$\frac{\text{Total Expenses on Schedule F (Line 35)}}{\text{Gross Income on Schedule F (Line 11)}}$$

If you have a farm and you incurred total expenses of $78,000 running your farm for the year and your gross income from the farm was $200,000, then your personal accounting ratio for Schedule F is computed as:

PAR(F)=78,000/200,000= 0.39 (or 39%)

Suppose that your farm lost a lot of money this year. Your expenses amounted to $120,000 while your gross income from the farm was only $20,000. In this case your personal accounting ratio for Schedule F is:

PAR(F)=
$$120,000/20,000= 6.00 \text{ (or 600\%)}$$

Again, a loss will make your PAR greater than 1.00.

Using Your PARs to Defeat the DIF

In the following chapter we present statistically-derived points that trigger the IRS's DIF to tag your return for audit. These are noted on the DIF-Buster Gauges for the different income tax Schedules. Use them as you would use the speedometer in your car. For each PAR there will be a "Caution Point" and a "Critical Point." We refer to the area after you exceed the Caution Point but before your ratio reaches the Critical Point as the "Caution Zone." The area of increasingly higher ratios beyond the Critical Point is referred to as the "Critical Zone." Once you pass the Caution Point and enter the Caution Zone, your probability of an audit increases as your ratio becomes greater. At the Critical Point, the IRS computer is known (from analysis of the data) to pick out your return to be audited. (Then, of course, the classifier will look at the return, so an audit is not a certainty even yet.)

CHAPTER 20

DIF-BUSTER GAUGES FOR SCHEDULES A, C, AND F

This is probably the most important chapter in this book. Over 90 percent of the audits in my sample (569 audited returns, out of a total of 631 audited returns) were determined to have been caused by the returns' exceeding the Critical Points for the PAR of either Schedule A, Schedule C, Schedule F (less than A and C), or combinations of any two of these schedules or all three of them. Incidentally, the big one is Schedule C.

Published statistics of the IRS indirectly confirm this fact. While the reported audit rate for all returns until this year has been roughly one percent, the audit rate for returns with a Schedule C has been four times as high, a close second were returns with a Schedule A, and at a somewhat lower rate but still more than double the overall percentage were returns with a Schedule F.

MOST AUDITS ARE CAUSED BY A RETURN REACHING OR EXCEEDING THE CRITICAL POINT FOR A PAR OF AT LEAST ONE OF THE THREE SCHEDULES: A, C, AND F

DIF-Buster Gauge for Schedule A:

Compute your personal accounting ratio for Schedule A as explained in the previous chapter. Now carry out the simple test below:

Is PAR(A) greater than or equal to 0.44 (or 44%)? If yes, you have just exceeded the critical point for Schedule A. The DIF-Formula inside the IRS computer will certainly kick out your return for possible audit.

THE CAUTION ZONE:

The caution zone for an audit based on PAR(A) is approached as your return gets close to having PAR(A) equal to 0.35 (35%).

Returns with PAR(A) less than 0.35 are not very likely to be audited; returns with PAR(A) between 0.35 and 0.44 have a relatively high audit probability (at least as far as computer-tagging); and returns with PAR(A) of above 0.44 are certain to be computer-tagged for audit. Figure 5 shows our DIF-Buster gauge for Schedule A.

DIF-Buster Gauge for Schedule C:

Compute your personal accounting ratio for Schedule C as explained in the previous chapter. Now carry out the simple test below:

Is PAR(C) greater than or equal to 0.63 (or 63%)? If yes, you have just exceeded the critical point for Schedule C. The DIF-Formula inside the IRS computer will certainly kick out your return for possible audit.

THE CAUTION ZONE:

The caution zone for an audit based on PAR(C) is approached as your return gets close to having PAR(A) equal to 0.52 (or 52%).

Figure 5: DIF-BUSTER GAUGE FOR SCHEDULE A

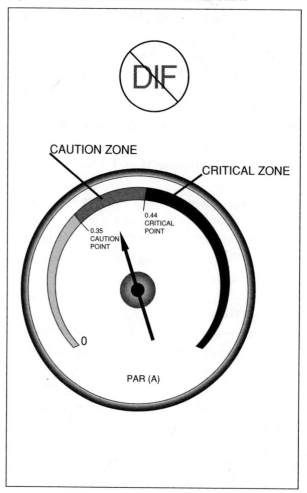

Returns with PAR(C) less than 0.52 are not very likely to be audited; returns with PAR(C) between 0.52 and 0.63 have a relatively high audit probability (at least as far as computer-tagging); and returns with PAR(C) of above 0.63 are certain to be computer-tagged for audit. Our Schedule C DIF-Buster gauge is shown in Figure 6.

DIF-Buster Gauge for Schedule F:

Compute your personal accounting ratio for Schedule F as explained in the previous chapter. Now carry out the simple test below:

Is PAR(F) greater than or equal to 0.67 (or 67%)? If yes, you have just exceeded the critical point for Schedule F. The DIF-Formula inside the IRS computer will certainly kick our your return for possible audit.

THE CAUTION ZONE:

The caution zone for an audit based on PAR(F) is approached as your return gets close to having PAR(F) equal to 0.56 (56%).

Returns with PAR(F) less than 0.56 are not very likely to be audited; returns with PAR(F) between 0.56 and 0.67 have a relatively high audit probability (at least as far as computer-tagging); and returns with PAR(F) of above 0.67 are certain to be computer-tagged for audit. Our DIF-Buster gauge for Schedule F is shown in Figure 7.

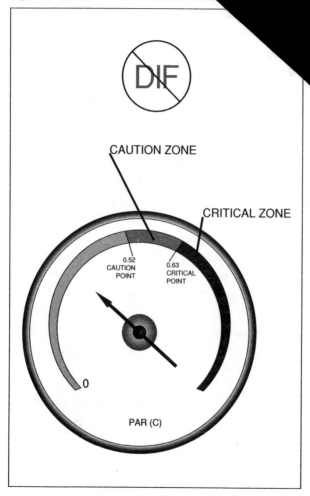

a Schedule A and a
mended for the combi-
ıe Caution Point is 1.03
ınation: PAR(C) + 1.5
st the inequality:
< 1.03 (or 103%, if
he two PARs)

satisfied, that is, if the com-
your PAR(C) to one-and-a-
critical point 1.03, the IRS

ARE PRESENT,
TEST EACH OF
THEM SEPARATELY
USING THE DIF-
BUSTING GAUGES
ABOVE, AND DO
THE COMBINATION
TEST.

computer may tag your ʌʌʌ urn for an audit (1.03 is the Caution Point for the combination). To be safe, you must check both the combination above and the separate tests for Schedules A and C given earlier.

Note that the separate tests above are more important than the combined test.

Figure 7: DIF-BUSTER GAUGE FOR SCHEDULE F

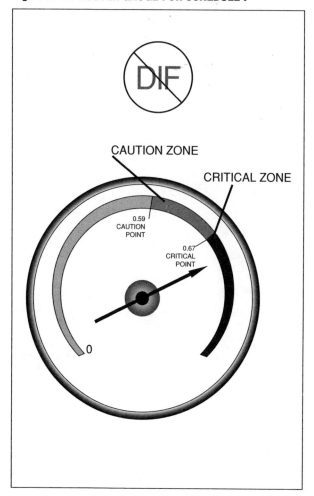

141

CHAPTER 21

USING THE DIF-BUSTER GAUGES, AND OTHER HINTS

The DIF-buster prescriptions in the previous chapter should be very useful for you in trying to audit-proof your tax return. Here is where the ideas of quality-control come in. When you prepare your tax return, compute the various PARs that are appropriate. Then check your PARs against the Caution Zone levels and the Critical Points. Suppose that your Schedule A PAR falls within the Caution Zone. This means that you have an increased chance of an audit based on the ratio of your total deductions on Schedule A as compared with your adjusted gross income. Now look carefully at all the items in your Schedule A. One of these items, or more than one, is the cause for this inflation of the PAR(A).

Once you have identified the cause, you have several alternatives. First, it may be that your entry on the schedule was simply in error, in which case correcting the error solves the problem. Assuming there is no error, you may want to include detailed explanations of the particular deductions that inflate the PAR. This way, when the IRS classifier looks at your return he or she will decide, hopefully, that the explanation and documentation you provided are satisfactory and you will not be audited. There is also another option, which may be viable in some situations. If

WHEN YOUR PAR FOR ONE OF THE SCHEDULES IS INFLATED (IN THE CAUTION OR THE CRITICAL ZONES), FIND WHICH ITEM (OR ITEMS) ON THE SCHEDULE IS THE CAUSE FOR THIS INFLATION

you have both a Schedule A and a Schedule C, perhaps you have included some expenses on your Schedule A that could have been listed legitimately on the Schedule C instead. For example, you listed office supplies used both as an employee of a company and for your side business on your Schedule A, and they could fit just as well on your Schedule C. If your PAR(A) will be reduced without affecting adversely your PAR(C), then shift the expense. Shifting items around may give you all the deductions to which you are entitled without breaching the limits on the PARs and thus getting you closer to an audit. Another policy, which may be used in conjunction with any of the others, is simply to file late—ask for an extension. This should help in reducing the audit probability.

What about other Schedules and Deductions?

SCHEDULE B:

In the analysis that traced the DIF used by the IRS, Schedule B did not come up as statistically significant. Two audits seem to have been caused by mismatched information provided on Schedule B. This does not mean that the DIF ignores Schedule B information. Schedule B lists interest and dividend income. All such income is very easily verifiable by the IRS—it is reported to the IRS by financial institutions. The caution here is a simple one: Be sure that what you claim as interest and dividends agrees completely with the information the IRS receives from other sources.

The IRS has special policies for its agents on how to deal with amended returns, that is, returns that are refiled after the original has been filed to report some newly discovered change in favor of the taxpayer. In dealing with amended returns, the IRS agent is instructed to audit any return with a decrease of $2,000 or more on Schedule B.

REFILING TO REDUCE INTEREST OR DIVIDEND INCOME BY $2,000 OR MORE WILL CAUSE AN AUDIT

SCHEDULE D:

Schedule D reports capital gains and losses. Here, too, all the information you report may be verified by the IRS based on information reported to it from other sources. This is why my sample did not contain any audits caused by Schedule D information. As with Schedule B, you should be careful that the information you provide is identical to what the IRS already knows about you.

BE SURE THAT WHAT YOU CLAIM AS CAPITAL GAINS/LOSSES AGREES COMPLETELY WITH THE INFORMATION THE IRS RECEIVES FROM OTHER SOURCES

Here, too, the IRS has additional strict rules for its agents on how to deal with amended returns that report a decrease in capital gains as compared with the originally filed return. An audit is mandated if the amounts involved are at least $10,000.

SCHEDULE E:

A number of people have asked me about Schedule E and how it affects audit probabilities. Surprisingly, Schedule E did not come up in the computer analysis as an important audit-causing element. Some returns with Schedule E expenses that were high as compared with income were not audited, others were audited. This

AN AMENDED
RETURN WITH A
DECREASE IN
CAPITAL GAINS OR
AN INCREASE IN
LOSS OF $10,000 OR
MORE WILL CAUSE
AN AUDIT

schedule is complicted, and many of the tax practitioners with whom I spoke agreed that they do not see many
Schedule E audits; some even suggested that the IRS
doesn't know how to handle this schedule. It would be
difficult for me to give you a simple gauge for this schedule, since there is no clear-cut picture as with Schedules
A, C, and F. A tentative Caution Point for this schedule
would be a ratio of about 0.60 (60% expenses as compared with income on this schedule). But again, this is
not a strong rule, just a rough guideline. When listing
rental property income on this schedule, watch out if
your rental property brought disproportionately low
income for its location, size, and value, as this is something the IRS likes to consider for audit.

Other Red Flags

1. BAD DEBT:

This is an item the IRS can question because it is easily
abused. Reporting an unrepayable debt may increase
your audit probability. Five audited returns in my sample reported bad debt. Only one unaudited return in my
sample reported bad debt.

2. CASUALTY LOSS:

This, too, is a questionable item that may cause the IRS to
audit your return. This will be especially true if you forget
to deduct $100.00 from the casualty amount, as required
by the tax code. None in my sample fell in this category.

3. MEDICAL EXPENSES LIMIT:

The tax code allows you to write off only medical expenses that exceed 7.5% of your adjusted gross income. Violating this rule may cause your return to be audited. The IRS is well aware of the potential for abuse of medical expense deductions. It is therefore important to be able to show that the medical expenses you claim were not paid by your insurance. Five returns in my sample were audited because the reported medical expenses did not exceed the required minimum percentage of the adjusted gross income.

4. CHARITABLE CONTRIBUTIONS:

"Excessive" charitable contributions reported on your return—that is, exceeding the limits provided by law—will make your return more likely to be audited. It is also very important to make sure that the contributions you deduct are to qualified charities as defined by law: religious, charitable, governmental, educational, and civic organizations recognized as legitimate recipients of tax-deductible contributions. The IRS is aware that tuition may be disguised as a charitable contribution and will look for such violations. The same is true if you report large donations of property, and the charitable organization reports to the IRS sale of these items at a value much lower than what you have claimed. Thirteen audited returns in my sample reported questionable charitable contributions. The audits, however, seem to have been caused by a combination of this factor with

BE SURE TO DOCUMENT THAT THE MEDICAL EXPENSES YOU CLAIM WERE NOT PAID BY YOUR MEDICAL INSURANCE CARRIER, AND THAT THEY EXCEED 7.5% OF YOUR ADJUSTED GROSS INCOME

MAKE SURE THE RECIPIENTS OF YOUR CHARITABLE CONTRIBUTIONS ARE LEGITIMATE AND THAT THE AMOUNTS ARE WITHIN THE LEGAL LIMIT

others. The data indicate, however, that returning charitable contributions of over ten percent of income received special attention.

5. HOME OFFICE:

This is an old favorite of the IRS. Home office expenses are reported on Schedule C and the PAR limits we discussed in that context apply. However, the fact that you report a home office may increase your audit probability somewhat beyond the limits we discussed for Schedule C, simply because the IRS likes to question the reasons for your having a home office in the first place. There have been many recent legal precedents, some in favor of the IRS, and an agent may be successful in disallowing your home office expenses if it can be argued that you are not entitled to one. Four hundred and eleven of my audits (over two-thirds of the audit sample) included a Schedule C. Of these returns, 289 reported a home office. Of the unaudited returns, 314 had a Schedule C, and 98 of them reported a home office. The audits, however, were all explained by breach of the PAR. I believe that a home office may increase your audit probability after your return has been picked by the DIF because you exceeded the PAR limit. Possibly, once this has happened, the classifier may be more likely to decide to audit you once he or she sees that you have reported a home office.

To Incorporate or Not to Incorporate?

Many professionals face the problem of whether to do business as individuals, filing their business income on Schedule C, or whether to incorporate. Clearly, many factors affect the decision to incorporate or not, and these factors should be looked at as a whole. From the point of view of the potential for a tax audit, the picture, at this time, is quite clear. The IRS loves to audit Schedule C. And it doesn't concern itself much with auditing small corporations. For corporations with assets less than $1 million, the audit rate in the last few years has been under two percent. For individuals filing Schedule C, on the other hand, the audit rate has been around five percent, and it is expected to rise this year. While reducing audit probability may not be the main reason to incorporate, it may still be a factor to consider.

CHAPTER 22

SUMMARY OF AUDIT-PROOFING RULES, AND EXAMPLES

The following is a summary of the things to look for on your return to try to minimize audit probability.

1. Check for math errors
2. No nice numbers
3. No significant inconsistencies across years
4. No large numerical shifts across years
5. Agreement of federal return with state return
6. No breach of legal limits on deductions
7. Explain all questionable items or amounts
8. File late if possible
9. Agreement of information with independent reporting
10. PAR(A) not in Critical Zone, and preferably not in Caution Zone
11. PAR(C) not in Critical Zone, and preferably not in Caution Zone
12. PAR(F) not in Critical Zone, and preferably not in Caution Zone
13. PAR(C) + 1.5 PAR(A) satisfying Caution inequality
14. Check for red flags: bad debt, casualty loss.

EXAMPLES

The following examples of tax returns are real. The names have been changed for obvious reasons. So have the professions, geographical locations, and other details. Small changes were also made in all the numbers involved so that even the IRS with its big computer will not be able to identify the actual taxpayers whose returns these are.

EXAMPLE (1)

John Greene is a realtor living in Omaha. He is married with no dependent children; his wife is retired. John's return is shown below. Was John's return audited?

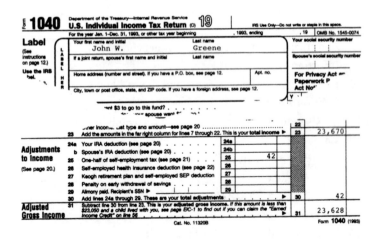

Schedule A—Itemized Deductions

(Schedule B is on back)

► Attach to Form 1040. ► See Instructions for Schedules A and B (Form 1040).

OMB No. 1545-0074

1994

Attachment
Sequence No. **07**

Name(s) shown on Form 1040

John W. Greene

Your social security number

Medical	1	Caution: ~~~ ·enses reimbursed or paid by oth~~ ~ (see page A-1' ~~		

| **Total Itemized Deductions** | 29 | Is Form 1040, line 32, over $111,800 (over $55,900 if married filing separately)? **NO.** Your deduction is not limited. Add the amounts in the far right column for lines 4 through 28. Also, enter on Form 1040, line 34, the **larger of** this amount or your standard deduction. **YES.** Your deduction may be limited. See page A-5 for the amount to enter. | ► | 29 | 8,409 |

Profit or Loss From Business

(Sole Proprietorship)

► **Partnerships, joint ventures, etc., must file Form 1065.**

► Attach to Form 1040 or Form 1041. ► See Instructions for Schedule C (Form 1040).

OMB No. 1545-0074

1994

Attachment
Sequence No. **09**

Name of proprietor

John W. Greene

Social security number (SSN)

A	Principal business or profession, including product or service (see page C-1)	**B** Enter principal business code (see page C-6) ►
C	Business name. If no separate business name, leave blank.	**D** Employer ID number (EIN), if any

E   Business address (including suite or room no.) ► ....
    City, town or post office, state, and ZIP code

F   Accounting method: (1) ☐ Cash   (2) ☐ Accrual   (3) ☐ Other (specify) ► ....

G   Method(s) used to value closing inventory: (1) ☐ Cost   (2) ☐ Lower of cost or market   (3) ☐ Other (attach explanation)   (4) ☐ Does not apply (if checked, skip line H)   Yes   No

H   Was there any change in determining quantities, costs, or valuations between opening and closing inventory? If "Yes," attach explanation . . . .

I   Did you "materially participate" in the operation of this business during 1994? If "No," see page C-2 for limit on losses. . . .

J   If you started or acquired this business during 1994, check here . . . . ► ☐

Part I   Income

1	Gross receipts or sales. **Caution:** If this income was reported to you on Form W-2 and the "Statutory employee" box on that form was checked, see page C-2 and check here . . . . ► ☐	1	
2	Returns and allowances	2	
3	Subtract line 2 from line 1	3	
4	Cost of goods sold (from line 40 on page 2)	4	
5	**Gross profit.** Subtract line 4 from line 3	5	
6	Other income, including Federal and state gasoline or fuel tax credit or refund (see page C-2) . . .	6	
7	**Gross income.** Add lines 5 and 6 . . . . ►	7	3,780

Part II   Expenses. Enter expenses for business use of your home **only** on line 30.

8	Advertising			(see page and profit-sharing plans			
a	Mortgage (paid to banks, etc.) .	16a		d Subtract line 24c from line 24b .	24d	
b	Other	16b		25 Utilities	25	
17	Legal and professional services	17		26 Wages (less employment credits) .	26	
18	Office expense	18		27 Other expenses (from line 46 on page 2)	27	2,163
28	**Total expenses** before expenses for business use of home. Add lines 8 through 27 in columns. . ►	28	3,182
29	Tentative profit (loss). Subtract line 28 from line 7	29	598
30	Expenses for business use of your home. Attach **Form 8829**	30	0
31	**Net profit or (loss).** Subtract line 30 from line 29. • If a profit, enter on **Form 1040, line 12,** and ALSO on **Schedule SE, line 2** (statutory employees, see page C-5). Estates and trusts, enter on Form 1041, line 3. • If a loss, you MUST go on to line 32.	31	598

32   If you have a loss, check the box that describes your investment in this activity (see page C-5).
     • If you checked 32a, enter the loss on **Form 1040, line 12,** and ALSO on **Schedule SE, line 2** (statutory employees). See page C-5). Estates and trusts, enter on Form 1041, line 3.
     • If you checked 32b, you MUST attach **Form 6198.**

32a ☐ All investment is at risk.
32b ☐ Some investment is not at risk.

For Paperwork Reduction Act Notice, see Form 1040 instructions.   Cat. No. 11334P   Schedule C (Form 1040) 1994

EXAMPLE (2)

Denise Burns is a civil engineer living with her husband Michael in New York City. Their return is shown below. Was this return audited?

Form **1040**	Department of the Treasury—Internal Revenue Service				
	U.S. Individual Income Tax Return (O) 19		IRS Use Only—Do not write or staple in this space.		
	For the year Jan. 1–Dec. 31, 1993, or other tax year beginning	, 1993, ending	, 19	OMB No. 1545-0074	

Label (See instructions on page 12.) L A B E L Use the IRS

	Your first name and initial	Last name		Your social security number
	Denise M.	Burns		
	If a joint return, spouse's first name and initial	Last name		Spouse's social security number

Home address (number and street). If you have a P.O. box, see page 12. | Apt. no. |

	21a	Social security benefits ⎣ 21a ⎦	b Taxable amount (see page ...)	22	1,905
	22	Other income. List type and amount—see page 20			
	23	Add the amounts in the far right column for lines 7 through 22. This is your **total income** ▶		23	49,926

Adjustments to Income (See page 20.)

	24a	Your IRA deduction (see page 20)	24a		
	b	Spouse's IRA deduction (see page 20)	24b		
	25	One-half of self-employment tax (see page 21) . . .	25	73	
	26	Self-employed health insurance deduction (see page 22)	26		
	27	Keogh retirement plan and self-employed SEP deduction	27		
	28	Penalty on early withdrawal of savings	28		
	29	Alimony paid. Recipient's SSN ▶	29		
	30	Add lines 24a through 29. These are your **total adjustments** . . . . ▶		30	73

Adjusted Gross Income

	31	Subtract line 30 from line 23. This is your **adjusted gross income**. If this amount is less than $23,050 and a child lived with you, see page EIC-1 to find out if you can claim the "Earned Income Credit" on line 56 . . . . ▶		31	49,853

For Paperwork Reduction Act Notice, see page 7. Cat. No. 11320B Form **1040** (1993)

SCHEDULES A&B (Form 1040)

Department of the Treasury Internal Revenue Service (O)

Schedule A—Itemized Deductions

(Schedule B is on back)

▶ Attach to Form 1040. ▶ See Instructions for Schedules A and B (Form 1040).

OMB No. 1545-0074

19

Attachment Sequence No. **07**

Name(s) shown on Form 1040 | Your social security number |
| Denise M. Burns | |

		include	...ed or paid		
	Mi...				
	24	Subtract line 23 from ... .. zero or less, enter -0-			

Other Miscellaneous Deductions

	25	Other—from list on page A-5. List type and amount ▶ .... ▶	25	

Total Itemized Deductions

	26	Is the amount on Form 1040, line 32, more than $108,450 (more than $54,225 if married filing separately)?		
		• **NO.** Your deduction is not limited. Add lines 4, 8, 12, 16, 17, 18, 24, and 25 and enter the total here. Also enter on Form 1040, line 34, the **larger** of this amount or your standard deduction.	26	6,461
		• **YES.** Your deduction may be limited. See page A-5 for the amount to enter.		

For Paperwork Reduction Act Notice, see Form 1040 instructions. | Cat. No. 11330X | Schedule A (Form 1040) 1993

Profit or Loss From Business

(Sole Proprietorship)

▶ Partnerships, joint ventures, etc., must file Form 1065.

▶ Attach to Form 1040 or Form 1041.   ▶ See Instructions for Schedule C (Form 1040).

19

Attachment
Sequence No. **09**

Name of proprietor   Denise M. Burns

Social security number (SSN)

A   ~ioal business or profession. including produ~* ~- ~~

	Legai ~ ~~ofessional services	17		2,241	~~.	Other expenses (from line 46 on	~~	~~
18	Office expense	18			27	page 2)	27	8,227
28	**Total expenses** before expenses for business use of home. Add lines 8 through 27 in columns. . ▶						28	44,407
29	Tentative profit (loss). Subtract line 28 from line 7						29	1,024
30	Expenses for business use of your home. Attach **Form 8829**						30	0
31	**Net profit or (loss).** Subtract line 30 from line 29.							
	• If a profit, enter on **Form 1040, line 12,** and ALSO on **Schedule SE, line 2** (statutory employees, see page C-5). Fiduciaries, enter on Form 1041, line 3.						31	1,024
	• If a loss, you MUST go on to line 32.							
32	If you have a loss, check the box that describes your investment in this activity (see page C-5).							
	• If you checked 32a, enter the loss on **Form 1040, line 12,** and ALSO on **Schedule SE, line 2** (statutory employees, see page C-5). Fiduciaries, enter on Form 1041, line 3.						32a ☐	All investment is at risk.
	• If you checked 32b, you MUST attach **Form 6198.**						32b ☐	Some investment is not at risk.

For Paperwork Reduction Act Notice, see Form 1040 instructions.   Cat. No. 11334P   Schedule C (Form 1040) 1993

Answers:

Both John and Denise were audited. John's PAR(C) is high: 84.2%, which is past the critical point of 63%. His PAR(A) is 35.6%, which is just at the start of the Caution Zone for PAR(A). The combined score is: PAR(C)+1.5PAR(A)=137.6%, which is also in the bad zone. Most likely, John's high PAR(C) is the cause of the audit. Denise's PAR(C) is 98%, way past the critical point, but her PAR(A) is in the safe zone at 13%. At 117.5%, her combined ratio is also in the bad zone. She was definitely audited only because of her high PAR(C).

EXAMPLE (3)

Dr. Michael Stern is a pediatrician living in Kansas City. His wife, Claire, is a fashion designer who works out of the couple's home. They have three children: Alan (8), Beth (6), and Dwayne (3 1/2). The Sterns' combined Adjusted Gross Income in 1993 was $366,512. They filed a joint return with two Schedules C: the one for Michael's practice showed an income of $248,579, with $22,588 in total expenses. Claire's business showed income of $172,520, and her claimed expenses totalled $31,676. The Sterns own a small 1-bedroom apartment in town, which they use as rental property, and list it on Schedule E. In 1993 they rented the unit for $12,120 and had upkeep expenses totalling $708. The Sterns own their home free and clear. In 1993 they contributed $8,330 to charity, none in the form of property. They had additional itemized deductions on Schedule A totalling $2,119. In 1989, the Sterns inherited a small farm 2 hours from Kansas City, where they spend weekends working the land growing cattle feed. The farm showed a small profit every year until 1992. In 1993, the farm income on Schedule F was $3,422, and the Sterns' farm expenses totalled $4,708.

In June 1995 the Sterns got a letter from the IRS asking them to call the District Office and schedule a meeting with an IRS agent who will begin an examination of their 1993 return. Claire exhaled deeply as she reread the letter for the third time. "Of course they want to audit us," she muttered, "we make too much money, Michael." Why were the Sterns audited? [The answer is in the next chapter.]

CHAPTER 23

FACTORS AFFECTING YOUR AUDIT PROBABILITY, AND MORE EXAMPLES

In preparing your tax return, I would recommend that you compute the PARs in the previous chapters, as well as check for other factors that can cause audits. If you can change things that are under your control, such as how much documentation you provide when you file, etc., you should definitely do so. Sometimes it may even be possible to legally shift expenses from one schedule to another. Shifting high expenses away from Schedule C may be enough to lower your PAR(C) to a level that is not in a dangerous zone. Such a shift may get you from the Critical Zone down to the Caution Zone, or maybe even out to the safe zone, while staying in the safe zone for other schedules. And the same holds for other schedules you file. Certain professionals, dentists and orthodontists for example, have a choice of where to deduct their operating expenses on Schedule C. One method may result in a lower PAR, thus improving their chance of avoiding an audit. If you can legally maintain your deductions and keep a low PAR, the reduced audit probability is certainly worth the effort. People in certain situations may decide that incorporating their business as an S-Corporation makes sense to them and this will give them the added bonus of a lower audit chance. There are other factors affecting your chance of winning the audit lottery. Where you live affects your chance of being audited.

We will start with the IRS's own reported overall audit probabilities by state for the last few years. These are given in Table 3 below. Find the appropriate number from the table that corresponds to your state. (If you live in Pennsylvania, your starting value is 0.69%, or 0.0069 if you like to write it decimally.) Now, since the IRS announced plans to increase the number of audits it conducts each year from about 1% nationwide to 2.21% nationwide, you need to multiply whatever number you get for your state in Table 4 by 2.21. (For Pennsylvania, your new audit probability this year will be 0.69% x 2.21=1.52%.)

AUDIT RATES VARY AROUND THE COUNTRY, BEING GENERALLY HIGHER IN THE WEST

Some books recommend that if you want to lower your audit probability you should move to a low-audit state. I find that to be a bit extreme. I like to consider the place you live as a given, whatever the audit probability there may be. Western states, in general, have a higher audit rate than other places. Ironically, I lived in a number of Western states for years, including five years in Alaska with its very high audit percentage, and never got audited. As soon as I moved to Boston, with its small audit rate, I got the letter from the IRS.

There are other factors you can't or won't change that affect your audit probability. In trying to show that their formula is more complex, the IRS acknowledged

TABLE 3: Audit-Probabilities by State (%)
Early 1990s (In Decreasing Order)

State	%	State	%
Alaska	2.46	Missouri	0.81
Nevada	1.89	Alabama	0.80
Wyoming	1.68	Indiana	0.77
Utah	1.61	Mississippi	0.77
Oklahoma	1.45	Oregon	0.77
N. Dakota	1.40	Vermont	0.77
Texas	1.36	Tennessee	0.76
California	1.31	Florida	0.74
Washington	1.20	S. Dakota	0.72
Montana	1.11	Connecticut	0.71
Colorado	1.07	Louisiana	0.71
Arizona	1.03	W. Virginia	0.71
Kansas	0.95	Pennsylvania	0.69
Idaho	0.94	Michigan	0.67
Hawaii	0.93	Virginia	0.64
Georgia	0.93	S. Carolina	0.64
Illinois	0.93	Arkansas	0.63
New Mexico	0.93	Kentucky	0.63
Ohio	0.90	New Jersey	0.62
Minnesota	0.89	Iowa	0.60
New York	0.89	N. Carolina	0.60
Delaware	0.86	New Hampshire	0.59
Nebraska	0.85	Wisconsin	0.59
Maryland (and	0.81	Massachusetts	0.58
District of Columbia)			
Rhode Island	0.57	Maine	0.55

(Compiled from: IRS Commissioner Annual Reports;
Statistics of Income Bulletin, IRS)

another of its often unfair reasons for putting taxpayers through the audit wringer: the number of children you have. My data set contained "average" numbers of dependents per return (0, 1, 2, 3, at the most 8), so I can't say that I saw how this rule is supposedly used by the agency in choosing people for audit, and I suspect that few audits are caused by this variable. But during one of my radio interviews, on WJJD in Chicago, a lady called in and described on the air how every single year she is audited by the IRS. She and her husband, apparently, make a modest living and don't file any "complicated" tax forms. They don't own a business or a farm; their charitable contributions are moderate; they don't have a home office. But they have 21 children. She described how every year her husband has to go downtown to meet with the IRS after receiving the letter asking them to come for an examination. You would think that after a few years of audits the IRS would have learned that this couple just has many children (it is their right, after all), and once they verified that all the children were real and indeed belonged to this family they would stop wasting taxpayer money on auditing them over and over again.

IF YOU HAVE 21 CHILDREN, COUNT ON BEING AUDITED EVERY YEAR

The senselessness of such audits brings us back to the main sources of high audit probability: large ratios of expenses to income on various schedules. Having looked at so many returns, I can say with confidence that high income alone does not cause audits. It is what you do with your money, and where your money comes from, that can cause audits. This point is demonstrated well with the solution of Example (3).

Answer to Example (3) in Chapter 22:

HIGH INCOME, BY ITSELF, DOES NOT CAUSE AN AUDIT

Ironically, the Sterns were not audited because of their high income. The PARs for the schedules where they made most of their money are all very low; almost everything else on their return looks good. What tripped up the Sterns was that tiny farm they inherited with its $1,286 loss, which brought their PAR(F) to 1.38, way inside the critical zone. This example demonstrates a typical problem with the IRS's method of choosing audits: the system looks for simple ratios of expenses to income. In this case, well-to-do taxpayers were audited, although it was a ratio of relatively small quantities that caused the audit. In other cases, people making a lot less money were audited, again because some ratios were high—even if the actual quantities forming the ratios, as well as the total income, were small, as demonstrated in the next example.

EXAMPLE (4):

Marian Delurgio is an instructor of human resource management at a local college in a suburb of New York City. Her teaching income in 1993 was $28,345.12. That year, Marian decided to try to supplement her income by doing some consulting in her area of expertise. The main problem was obtaining clients for her service, and Marian had to invest some time and effort, as well as money, in getting these clients. She did get one client, who paid her a fee of $750. Marian considered her efforts an investment in her future, expecting relatively high initial costs for advertising, setting up an office, and entertaining potential clients in anticipation of larger contracts in years to come. Elements of her Schedule C for 1993 are shown below.

Marian Delurgio Schedule C for 1993:

Line 7:	Gross Income	$750
Line 18:	Office Expenses	$935
Line 24:	Travel, Meals, and Entertainment	$826
Line 24 d:	Less 20%	$661
Line 28:	Total Expenses	$1,596

Was Marian Delurgio audited? You would think that such small amounts should be of no interest to the IRS, and that they would be wise to leave her alone and go after bigger fish. But no, since ratios are the name of the game and here we have PAR(C)=$1,596/$750=2.128 —a very high ratio, well in the Critical Zone—they did audit her. And they spent a lot of your money on an audit that is still ongoing but one that will likely result in no change in Marian's tax liability (and even if there was to be a change, how much could they get out of her?).

Cases such as this one demonstrate how inadequate the whole IRS system for selecting audits really is, and even more, they show the bad effect ratio-based audits have on our economy as a whole. For the very existence of such audits stifles growth and discourages entrepreneurship—the essence of American ingenuity and prosperity. When Marian tells her friends about the unpleasant and lengthy audit she had to endure (regardless of the outcome) just because she tried to develop her career, took a chance on herself and set up a consulting business, the story of her ordeal will discourage others from trying. And we are all worse off for it. A tax system that discourages development and economic progress is not worth having around. It is a system that is short-sighted, for it probably brings in billions of dollars in added tax revenues now but prevents businesses from growing—something that would bring trillions in future, direct tax revenues as these businesses become prosperous and productive.

Collier, Sarner and Associates, Inc., is a prominent firm specializing in tax advice for doctors and medical professionals. Their April 1 and April 15, 1995, newsletters quoted extensively from the first edition of this book. After describing my PAR's and their use in warning of high audit probability, Mr. Collier wrote in the newsletter that finally an explanation had been given—indirectly—for a well-known phenomenon involving doctors and audits. He wrote that tax attorneys could never quite figure out why young doctors tended to get audited much more frequently than older, established

RATIO-BASED IRS AUDITS STIFLE ECONOMIC GROWTH AND HURT THE NATION IN THE LONG RUN

**CURRENT IRS
AUDIT POLICY
HURTS
PROFESSIONALS
IN EARLY STAGES
OF THEIR
CAREERS**

doctors who made a lot more money. Now the mystery is solved, Collier said. Young doctors embarking on their careers have high expenses since they have to invest in building up their practice. In this stage of their professional lives, they have low incomes and high expenses, giving them high PAR(C) values, and this causes their audits. Older doctors make a lot of money and their practice is well-established. With high incomes and low expenses, these doctors have low PAR(C) values and, therefore, get audited less frequently. What can you say about a government policy that results in going after young professionals, hampering their growth and at best getting paltry sums in additional revenues, instead of allowing these productive members of society to develop their businesses unimpeded?

I am often asked if I have studied the separate effects on the audit probability of the various line items that enter into the PARs and whether these have a separate effect. The answer is yes and no. Yes, I did look at these effects, and no, I did not find that these items have an effect on audit probability that is separate from and not measured by the PAR itself. You don't need to worry about a ratio of charitable contributions to adjusted gross income (AGI), or a ratio of medical expenses to AGI, or a ratio of state and local taxes to AGI. All of these factors are measured together, as a whole, when you compute your PAR(A) the way I defined it. The returns I analyzed all tell the same story: check the PAR values against my gauges. The IRS computer will choose you for audit if you are in the Critical Zone for at least one schedule. Your audit probability already becomes significant as you get inside the Caution Zone. As far as audit probability goes, it doesn't matter what factor on your return got you there, whether it is charitable contributions on Schedule A or office expenses on Schedule C. It is the PAR(A), PAR(C), or PAR(F) that matters. Once you have found that you are in a Danger Zone for one or more of the schedules, you will definitely want to identify the particular item that caused that inflation and do something about it, such as supply an explanation with your return, or shift things around. But your audit selection by the computer is wholly determined by the PARs. In terms of importance, PAR(C) causes most audits, followed by PAR(A) and PAR(F). And a PAR(E) may have a small effect as well. So to summarize, what you want to watch out for in preparing your tax return is:

C A F E

Now E is not too important so we can drop that letter; winning the IRS game calls for you to

DECAF!

Here is one last example of an audited return with a Schedule C. It should be simple for you to figure out why this return was audited.

FORM 1040	Department of the Treasury – Internal Revenue Service	U.S. Individual Income Tax Return (t)	1993		

IRS Use Only - Do not write or staple in this space.

For the year Jan. 1 - Dec. 31, 1993, or other tax year beginning _____, 1993, ending _____, 19 _____   OMB No. 1545-0074

Label

(See instructions on page 12.)

Use the IRS label. Otherwise, please print or type.

L A B E L H E R E	Your first name and initial	Last name	Your social security number
	If a joint return, spouse's first name and initial	Last name	Spouse's social security number
	Home address (number and street). If you have a P.O. box, see page 12.	Apt. no.	**For Privacy Act and Paperwork Reduction Act Notice, see page 4.**
	City, town or post office, state, and ZIP code. If you have a foreign address, see page 12.		

Presidential Election Campaign (See page 12.)

	Yes	No	Note: Checking "Yes" will not change your tax or reduce your refund.
Do you want $3 to go to this fund?	X		
If a joint return, does your spouse want $3 to go to this fund?	X		

Filing Status

(See page 12.)

Check only one box.

1 ☐ Single
2 ☒ Married filing joint return (even if only one had income)
3 ☐ Married filing separate return. Enter spouse's soc. sec. no. above & full name here ▶
4 ☐ Head of household (with qualifying person). (See page 13.) If the qualifying person is a child but not your dependent, enter this child's name here ▶
5 ☐ Qualifying widow(er) with dependent child (year spouse died ▶ 19 ____). (See page 13.)

Exemptions

(See page 13.)

6a ☒ Yourself. If your parent (or someone else) can claim you as a dependent on his or her tax return, do not check box 6a. But be sure to check the box on line 33b on page 2 . . . }

No. of boxes checked on 6a and 6b   **2**

b ☒ Spouse.

c Dependents:

(1) Name (first, initial, and last name)	(2) Check if under age 1	(3) If age 1 or older, dependent's social security number	(4) Dependent's relationship to you	(5) No. of mos. lived in home in '93
•			SON	12
•			SON	12

No. of your children on 6c who:
• lived with you   **2**
• didn't live with you due to divorce or separation (see page 13)

Dependents on 6c not entered above

If more than six dependents, see page 14.

d If your child didn't live with you but is claimed as your dep. under pre-1985 agreement, check . . ▶ ☐

Add numbers entered on lines above ▶   **4**

e Total number of exemptions claimed.

Income

Attach Copy B of your Forms W-2, W-2G, and 1099-R here.

If you did not get a W-2, see page 10.

If you are attaching a check or money order, put it on top of any Forms W-2, W-2G, or 1099-R.

7	Wages, salaries, tips, etc. Attach Form(s) W-2.	7	
8a	Taxable interest income (see page 16). Attach Schedule B if over $400	8a	5,629
b	Tax-exempt interest income (see pg. 17). DON'T include on line 8a	8b	
9	Dividend income. Attach Schedule B if over $400	9	525
10	Taxable refunds, credits, or offsets of state and local income taxes (see page 17).	10	
11	Alimony received.	11	
12	Business income or (loss). Attach Schedule C or C-EZ.	12	3,907
13	Capital gain or (loss). Attach Schedule D.	13	3,711
14	Capital gain distributions not reported on line 13 (see page 17).	14	
15	Other gains or (losses). Attach Form 4797. FORM 4684	15	−1,500
16a	Total IRA distributions	16a	b Taxable amount (pg. 18)	16b	
17a	Total pensions and annuities.	17a	b Taxable amount (pg. 18)	17b	
18	Rental real estate, royalties, partnerships, S corporations, trusts, etc. Attach Schedule E.	18	
19	Farm income or (loss). Attach Schedule F.	19	
20	Unemployment compensation (see page 19).	20	
21a	Social security benefits	21a	b Taxable amount (pg. 19)	21b	
22	Other income.	22	
23	Add the amounts in the far right column for lines 7 through 22. This is your total income ▶	23	12,272

Adjustments to Income

(See page 20.)

24a	Your IRA deduction (see page 20).	24a		
b	Spouse's IRA deduction (see page 20).	24b		
25	One-half of self-employment tax (see page 21)	25	276	
26	Self-employed health insurance deduction (see page 22).	26	1,316	
27	Keogh retirement plan and self-employed SEP deduction	27		
28	Penalty on early withdrawal of savings	28		
29	Alimony paid. Recipient's SSN ▶	29		
30	Add lines 24a through 29. These are your total adjustments. ▶		30	1,592

Adjusted Gross Income

31	Subtract line 30 from 23. This is your adjusted gross income. If amount is less than $23,060 & a child lived w/ you, see pg. EIC-1 to find out if you can claim "Earned Income Credit" on line 56. ▶	31	10,680

Form **1040** (1993)

168

Schedule A—Itemized Deductions

(Schedule B is on back)

▶ **Attach to Form 1040.** ▶ **See Instructions for Schedules A and B (Form 1040).**

OMB No. 1545-0074

1994

Attachment
Sequence No. **07**

Name(s) shown on Form 1040

Your social security number

Medical and Dental Expenses		Caution: *Do not include expenses reimbursed or paid by others.*			
	1	Medical and dental expenses (see page A-1)	**1** 7,348		
	2	Enter amount from Form 1040, line 32. **2** 10,680			
	3	Multiply line 2 above by 7.5% (.075)	**3** 801		
	4	Subtract line 3 from line 1. If line 3 is more than line 1, enter -0-		**4**	6,547
Taxes You Paid (See page A-1.)	5	State and local income taxes	**5** 326		
	6	Real estate taxes (see page A-2)	**6** 1,700		
	7	Personal property taxes	**7**		
	8	Other taxes. List type and amount ▶	**8**		
	9	Add lines 5 through 8		**9**	2,026
Interest You Paid (See page A-2.)	10	Home mortgage interest and points reported to you on Form 1098	**10** 4,008		
	11	Home mortgage interest not reported to you on Form 1098. If paid to the person from whom you bought the home, see page A-3 and show that person's name, identifying no., and address ▶	**11**		
Note: Personal interest is not deductible.	12	Points not reported to you on Form 1098. See page A-3 for special rules	**12**		
	13	Investment interest. If required, attach Form 4952. (See page A-3.)	**13**		
	14	Add lines 10 through 13		**14**	4,008
Gifts to Charity If you made a gift and got a benefit for it, see page A-3.	15	Gifts by cash or check. If any gift of $250 or more, see page A-3	**15** 1,300		
	16	Other than by cash or check. If any gift of $250 or more, see page A-3. If over $500, you **MUST** attach Form 8283	**16**		
	17	Carryover from prior year	**17**		
	18	Add lines 15 through 17		**18**	1,300
Casualty and Theft Losses	19	Casualty or theft loss(es). Attach Form 4684. (See page A-4.)		**19**	0
Job Expenses and Most Other Miscellaneous Deductions (See page A-5 for expenses to deduct here.)	20	Unreimbursed employee expenses—job travel, union dues, job education, etc. If required, you **MUST** attach Form 2106 or 2106-EZ. (See page A-5.) ▶	**20**		
	21	Tax preparation fees	**21** 150		
	22	Other expenses—investment, safe deposit box, etc. List type and amount ▶	**22**		
	23	Add lines 20 through 22	**23** 150		
	24	Enter amount from Form 1040, line 32. **24** 10,680			
	25	Multiply line 24 above by 2% (.02)	**25** 214		
	26	Subtract line 25 from line 23. If line 25 is more than line 23, enter -0-		**26**	0
Other Miscellaneous Deductions	27	Moving expenses incurred before 1994. Attach Form 3903 or 3903-F. (See page A-5.)	**27**		
	28	Other—from list on page A-5. List type and amount ▶		**28**	0
Total Itemized Deductions	29	Is Form 1040, line 32, over $111,800 (over $55,900 if married filing separately)? **NO.** Your deduction is not limited. Add the amounts in the far right column for lines 4 through 28. Also, enter on Form 1040, line 34, the **larger** of this amount or your standard deduction. ▶ **YES.** Your deduction may be limited. See page A-5 for the amount to enter.		**29**	13,881

For Paperwork Reduction Act Notice, see Form 1040 instructions.

Cat. No. 11330X

Schedule A (Form 1040) 1994

SCHEDULE C
(Form 1040)

Department of the Treasury
Internal Revenue Service   (X)

Profit or Loss From Business
(Sole Proprietorship)

▶ Partnerships, joint ventures, etc., must file Form 1065.

▶ Attach to Form 1040 or Form 1041.   ▶ See Instructions for Schedule C (Form 1040).

OMB No. 1545-0074

1994

Attachment
Sequence No. **09**

Name of proprietor | Social security number (SSN)

A Principal business or profession, including product or service (see page C-1) VENDING	B Enter principal business code (see page C-6) ▶ 9 8 3 7
C Business name. If no separate business name, leave blank.	D Employer ID number (EIN), if any

E Business address (including suite or room no.) ▶ ....
  City, town or post office, state, and ZIP code

F Accounting method: (1) ☒ Cash (2) ☐ Accrual (3) ☐ Other (specify) ▶ ....

				Yes	No
G Method(s) used to value closing inventory: (1) ☒ Cost (2) ☐ Lower of cost or market (3) ☐ Other (attach explanation) (4) ☐ Does not apply (if checked, skip line H)					
H Was there any change in determining quantities, costs, or valuations between opening and closing inventory? If "Yes," attach explanation					X
I Did you "materially participate" in the operation of this business during 1994? If "No," see page C-2 for limit on losses. . .				x	
J If you started or acquired this business during 1994, check here . . . . ▶ ☐					

Part I Income

1	Gross receipts or sales. **Caution:** If this income was reported to you on Form W-2 and the "Statutory employee" box on that form was checked, see page C-2 and check here . . . . ▶ ☐	1	572,594
2	Returns and allowances	2	
3	Subtract line 2 from line 1	3	572,594
4	Cost of goods sold (from line 40 on page 2)	4	167,303
5	**Gross profit.** Subtract line 4 from line 3	5	405,291
6	Other income, including Federal and state gasoline or fuel tax credit or refund (see page C-2) . . .	6	3,221
7	**Gross income.** Add lines 5 and 6 . . . . ▶	7	408,512

Part II Expenses. Enter expenses for business use of your home **only** on line 30.

8	Advertising	8		19 Pension and profit-sharing plans	19	
9	Bad debts from sales or services (see page C-3) .	9		20 Rent or lease (see page C-4):		
				a Vehicles, machinery, and equipment .	20a	
10	Car and truck expenses (see page C-3)	10		b Other business property . .	20b	
11	Commissions and fees. .	11		21 Repairs and maintenance . .	21	2,550
12	Depletion	12		22 Supplies (not included in Part III) .	22	7,386
13	Depreciation and section 179 expense deduction (not included in Part III) (see page C-3) . .	13		23 Taxes and licenses	23	18,911
				24 Travel, meals, and entertainment:		
				a Travel	24a	
14	Employee benefit programs (other than on line 19) . . .	14		b Meals and entertainment .		
15	Insurance (other than health) .	15		c Enter 50% of line 24b subject to limitations (see page C-4) .		
16	Interest:					
a	Mortgage (paid to banks, etc.) .	16a		d Subtract line 24c from line 24b	24d	
b	Other	16b		25 Utilities	25	6,045
17	Legal and professional services	17		26 Wages (less employment credits) .	26	51,590
18	Office expense	18		27 Other expenses (from line 46 on page 2)	27	

28	**Total expenses** before expenses for business use of home. Add lines 8 through 27 in columns. . ▶	28	404,605
29	Tentative profit (loss). Subtract line 28 from line 7	29	3,907
30	Expenses for business use of your home. Attach **Form 8829**	30	
31	Net profit or (loss). Subtract line 30 from line 29.		
	• If a profit, enter on **Form 1040, line 12,** and ALSO on **Schedule SE, line 2** (statutory employees, see page C-5). Estates and trusts, enter on Form 1041, line 3.	31	3,907
	• If a loss, you MUST go on to line 32.		

32 If you have a loss, check the box that describes your investment in this activity (see page C-5).
  • If you checked 32a, enter the loss on **Form 1040, line 12,** and ALSO on **Schedule SE, line 2** (statutory employees, see page C-5). Estates and trusts, enter on Form 1041, line 3.
  • If you checked 32b, you MUST attach **Form 6198.**

32a ☐ All investment is at risk.
32b ☐ Some investment is not at risk.

For Paperwork Reduction Act Notice, see Form 1040 instructions.   Cat. No. 11334P   Schedule C (Form 1040) 1994

CHAPTER 24

TAX SHELTERS

Atax shelter is a method or transaction or investment that gives tax benefits to the participant. The IRS code is designed to give us the opportunity to benefit from legitimate tax shelters—those that have redeeming social and/or economic value as recognized by Congress. The idea behind the law is to encourage certain kinds of investments even though the government pays for them by having reduced tax revenues. Your home is a tax shelter, since your mortgage interest and taxes are deductible. Many tax shelters are business ventures in which accounting losses far exceed the accounting income. The losses are then used to offset other income and thus shield it from taxation. Our economy requires large investments in farming, mining, oil and gas drilling, building, etc., and the purpose of the law reducing the tax is to allow the formation of such businesses that require large initial investment. Tax shelters usually have at least one of the following characteristics:

1. Taxes are deferred to later years.
2. Ordinary gains are converted to capital gains.
3. Leverage is used.

Clearly, there is great potential for abuse. An abusive tax shelter, as the IRS defines it, is a scheme that involves artificial transactions with little or no economic value, and whose sole purpose is to reduce the participant's tax bill. Often an abusive tax shelter will involve a package deal that is designed from the start to generate losses, deductions, or credits.

THE IRS VIGOROUSLY HUNTS DOWN ABUSIVE TAX SHELTERS

A number of the audits in my sample seem to have been picked up because the taxpayer participated in an abusive tax shelter. The IRS also likes to make an example of people participating in such tax shelters. In a crackdown on abusive tax shelters a few years ago, a number of Hollywood personalities were investigated and penalized for participating in one such scheme. Often these schemes are marketed in a way that hides their true nature, and you will want to be careful before you invest.

YOU DO NOT WANT TO HAVE A TAX SHELTER THAT THE IRS WILL THINK IS AN ABUSIVE ONE

It is very unlikely that the DIF itself has some mechanism that can identify an abusive tax shelter as opposed to a legitimate one. In most probability, it is the classifier who looks at your return once it is identified by the DIF for other reasons, who will suspect an abusive tax shelter and make the decision to audit you. Remember that it really doesn't matter whether or not your tax shelter is abusive. What counts is what the IRS agent or classifier will think it is, and that will determine whether or not you are audited.

What does the IRS look for in determining that a tax shelter is abusive? IRS agents are trained to look for the following telltales in checking for abusive tax shelters:

1. Investments made late in the tax year.
2. A very large portion of the investment is made in the first year.
3. Burden and benefit of ownership is not passed to the taxpayer.
4. The sale price does not compare well with fair market value.
5. Estimated present value of future income does not compare well with present value of all investment and associated costs.

According to the IRS, most abusive tax shelters are in the following areas: real estate, oil and gas, farming, motion pictures, videotapes, commodities, master recordings, leasing, cable TV, mining, foreign trusts. The IRS has a special Tax Shelter Program designed to combat abusive tax shelters. You will want to be very careful in preparing your return to avoid falling into the category of people audited for tax shelter abuse. Audits of tax shelter abuse result in an average annual additional tax collection of over 2.5 billion dollars.

As a final quality-control check of your return before submitting it, check for the above signs that the IRS considers significant in determining that a tax shelter is abusive. If you have investments in any of the areas listed above, and if your investment has any of the features that auditors look for, you will do well to include ample documentation to explain the investment so the classifier does not decide to audit you.

CHAPTER 25

A WAY (FOR SOME) TO HAVE A FINAL LAUGH

When you file your tax return you sign a statement saying that, under penalty of perjury, you have told the truth as accurately as possible. The following should only be interpreted in this context.

Suppose that you filed your return, as accurately as possible at the time of filing, but later discovered that you left out some item or items that would reduce your tax liability. To take advantage of these new facts, you want to refile your tax return. This is possible, and such a return is called an amended return, and is filed on Form 1040X. An amended return is also possible in case you have been audited and as a result of your audit you were charged additional tax. Regardless of whether or not you appealed, you ended up paying that additional tax. Now, some time later, you discover new facts and evidence that you believe will entitle you to deductions that the auditor had disallowed. You may now file an amended return to recover your money.

The first fact we need to mention is that, in general, filing an amended return will increase your probability of an audit. For some reason, the IRS looks at amended returns more sternly. The Service believes that more abuse may be possible with amended returns and instructs its agents to audit these more often. The two rules mentioned in a previous chapter about decreases in tax liability beyond certain limits for schedules B and D requiring an audit are good examples of this policy.

IN GENERAL, FILING AN AMENDED RETURN INCREASES YOUR CHANCE OF AN AUDIT OF YOUR ORIGINAL RETURN

There is a more important point here, however, which works very strongly in your favor. This point—as is the case with many topics in this book—has to do with time. For some odd reason, an aberration in the tax law exists. The period of time for the IRS to collect more tax from you expires, as we said earlier, after three years from the date the tax was due (usually April 15th of the year you file, although note our earlier comments on the exceptions). Now, your time period for requesting a refund for a particular tax year is also three years from the time you filed (assuming you filed on April 15), regardless of any extensions you may have obtained. There are two exceptions to this rule. First, if your revision involves a bad debt or a worthless security, you have up to seven years to file an amended return. Second, you may file for a refund up to two years from the last date tax was paid for the year, but the refund amount is limited to no more than the amount of tax paid on that latest date. For example, if you were audited and had to pay more tax, say two years after filing, you can file for a refund up to two years from that last date you paid tax (that is, four years since the original return was filed), but the amount of refund is limited to the amount of tax you paid at that latest date.

Here comes your incredible advantage. While you have all this time to file for a refund, the IRS is still limited by the time limit valid for your original return and cannot ask you for more tax for the year once the original time limit of three years has expired.

Suppose you filed your return for 1994 on April 15, 1995, and a few months later discovered that you failed to make a deduction that would have reduced your tax for 1994 by several thousand dollars. The best thing for you to do is to wait until a few days before April 15, 1998 (that is, a few days before time runs out on you for requesting a refund) and then file an amended return for 1994 claiming the deduction. The IRS may disallow your claim, or reduce the amount, or it may pay you in full. At any rate, once April 15, 1998 arrives, it cannot ask you for more tax for 1994 because the period of limitations will have expired. Filing a few days before April 15, 1998, puts you

WHILE YOU MAY ASK FOR A REFUND UP TO THREE YEARS AFTER FILING YOUR ORIGINAL RETURN, THE IRS MAY NOT DEMAND MORE TAX FOR THAT YEAR ONCE THREE YEARS HAVE ELAPSED

Figure 8: The Time Element and Amended Returns

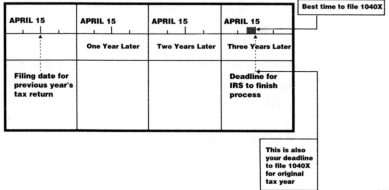

177

**BY TIMING
YOUR REQUEST
FOR A REFUND
CLEVERLY YOU CAN
MAKE IT ALMOST
IMPOSSIBLE FOR
THE IRS TO AUDIT
YOUR ORIGINAL
RETURN AND ASK
FOR MORE TAX**

within the time limit for a refund, and yet makes it almost impossible for the IRS to audit your 1994 return and ask for more tax—all in a few days before the deadline passes. This is demonstrated in Figure 8.

Out of 58 amended returns in my sample, 39 were audited. Of the nineteen unaudited amended returns, seven were filed within two months of the date time would have run out on the IRS for conducting an audit of the amended return.

This technique can also be used quite well after an audit. You pay the additional tax assessed in the audit (assuming you were unable to reverse the assessment in appeals or court), you wait for the time to run out completely on the IRS for asking for more tax—three years from the time you filed—but no later than two years after the audit. Then you file for a refund. This assumes that you can present some newly discovered reason for asking for the refund: something in your favor that was overlooked in the audit, or something that does not have to do with the audit—some other item or items in the original return. The IRS cannot audit you again, because the period allowing it to ask for more tax for that year is over. In such cases, the maximum amount you may claim as refund is the last amount of tax paid, the additional tax assessed in the audit.

Of the returns in my sample, none were assessed more tax or even audited if the amended return was filed within two weeks of the day time ran out on the IRS to assess more tax. Remember that the amended return itself may not result in the amount of refund you request, but timing will minimize exposure of the rest of your return to an audit. Playing the amended return game can be dangerous and tricky, but to the shrewd and lucky it can be quite rewarding.

CHAPTER 26

APPENDIX—THE TAXPAYER BILL OF RIGHTS

Enacted by Congress in 1988, the Taxpayer Bill of Rights is designed to offer some protection to us taxpayers against the all-powerful Goliath. This chapter summarizes some of the more important rights provided by the law. The most important protection in the bill is the establishment of an Ombudsman to protect the taxpayers. Usually, the Ombudsman works through the IRS' Problem Resolution Offices that are part of each District Office. Here, problems with the Service may be worked out. The Ombudsman may issue a Taxpayer Assistance Order (TAO), which can stop the seizure of property or wages. To get a TAO, the taxpayer must apply to the Problem Resolution Office and show that significant hardship will result from the IRS action. Other important rights are:

1. A Notice of Taxpayer's Rights must be mailed to the taxpayer with the first IRS notice about delinquent taxes. This is an important publication.

2. Taxpayers' Rights during non-criminal IRS interviews are:
   a) The right to make an audio recording of the interview. The taxpayer must notify the agent that a

recording is being made and give the IRS a chance to do the same.

b) A taxpayer may send a qualified representative to meet with the agent instead of him- or herself.

c) At any time during the interview, the taxpayer may request an end to the meeting to have an opportunity to consult with a tax professional.

d) The IRS is now required to consider the taxpayer when setting times and places for interviews.

3. If a taxpayer relied on bad IRS written advice, penalties may be removed.

4. IRS production quotas are officially forbidden. This means that the auditor's performance is not supposed to be evaluated based on the amount of tax dollars he or she collects.

5. A taxpayer may propose to the IRS an installment payment plan. However, the IRS is not obligated to accept the plan, only to consider it.

6. A Notice of Levy must be given to the taxpayer prior to property seizure, giving the taxpayer 30 days to contest or negotiate to stop the levy.

7. Erroneous tax liens may be appealed to the Ombudsman.

8. The taxpayer has the right to sue the IRS for up to $100,000 plus legal costs if IRS collection personnel have intentionally disregarded the law. Stringent provisions, however, apply to protect the IRS.

YOU CAN HELP!

Monumental research has gone into developing this book. The crucial element was the collection of tax returns of audited versus unaudited taxpayers. Future editions of this book will depend on the availability of ample new data.

If you have been audited in recent years, I would greatly appreciate receiving a copy of your audited return.

To reward your participation, I will run your present year return through the computer program and tell you what to watch out for.

Please send your audited return to:

Professor Amir D. Aczel
Department of Mathematical Sciences
Bentley College
Waltham, MA 02154

Thank you!

Aczel, Amir D., *Complete Business Statistics*, 3rd ed., Burr Ridge, Ill.: Irwin, 1996. (Chapter 16 of my book gives a thorough explanation of discriminant analysis.)

Aczel, Amir D. "On an IRS Maga-Plan for Costly and Unnecessary Random Audits," *Taxes* Magazine, August 1995, pp. 461-2.

American Statistical Association, *Proceedings of the Joint Statistical Meetings*, San Francisco. Arlington, VA: American Statistical Association, 1993. (Various papers by IRS statisticians.)

Bernstein, Allen, *Tax Guide for College Teachers*, Washington, DC: Academic Information Service, 1992.

Burnham, David, *A Law Unto Itself: Power, Politics, and the IRS*, New York: Random House, 1990. (The title says it all.)

Commerce Clearing House Tax Law Editors, *Federal Tax Course*, Chicago, IL: Commerce Clearing House, 1990.

Daily, Frederick W., *Winning the IRS Game: How Anyone Can Beat the IRS*, San Francisco: Dropzone Press, 1991. (A tax attorney reveals some of his trade secrets.)

Diogenes, *The April Game: Secrets of an Internal Revenue Agent*, Chicago: The Playboy Press, 1973.

Gates, Bryan E., *How to Represent Your Client Before the IRS*, New York: McGraw-Hill, 1983. (A guide to tax professionals, with useful advice.)

Huberty, Carl J., *Applied Discriminant Analysis*, New York: Wiley, 1994. (An excellent guide to understanding discriminant analysis.)

Internal Revenue Service Commissioner's *Annual Report*, Washington, DC: U.S. Department of the Treasury, 1991.

Internal Revenue Service Commissioner's *Annual Report*, Washington, DC: U.S. Department of the Treasury, 1992.

Internal Revenue Service, *Statistics of Income Bulletin*, Washington, DC: U.S. Department of the Treasury, Vol. 13, Numbers 1 and 2, 1993.

Internal Revenue Service, *Statistics of Income Bulletin*, Washington, DC: U.S. Department of the Treasury, Vol. 12, Number 1, 1992.

Internal Revenue Service, *Your Federal Income Tax: for Individuals* (Publication 17), Washington, DC: U.S. Department of the Treasury, 1993. (The IRS's guide for individuals preparing their taxes.)

Larson, Martin A., *The IRS vs. the Middle Class*, Old Greenwich, Conn.: Devin-Adair, 1980.

Lasser, J. K., *Your Income Tax*, New York: Prentice-Hall, 1993. (A classic guide for preparing your taxes.)

McCormally, Kevin, *Sure Ways to Cut Your Taxes*, Washington DC: Kiplinger, 1994. (A friendly, sometimes humorous guide to preparing your taxes.)

Norusis, Marija J., SPSS *Advanced Statistics Guide*, Chicago: SPSS, 1990. (A statistical guide to computing a discriminant function, such as the IRS' "DIF".)

Phillips, Lawrence C., and John L. Kramer, eds., *Federal Taxation*, New York: Prentice-Hall, 1990.

Schnepper, Jeff A., I*nside IRS: How Internal Revenue Works (You Over)*, New York: Stein and Day, 1978.

Schnepper, Jeff A., *How to Pay Zero Taxes*, New York: McGraw-Hill, 1994. (A good guide to federal taxation, notwithstanding its misleading title.)

Stern, Philip M., *The Rape of the Taxpayer*, New York: Random House, 1973.

Sydlaske, Janet M., and Richard K. Millcroft, *The Only Tax Audit Guide You'll Ever Need*, New York: Wiley, 1990. (Advice on handling your audit.)

Tax Notes, an independent weekly newsletter covering all issues of taxation, with excellent articles about IRS policies by George Guttman.

Wade, Jack W., *Audit-Proofing Your Return*, New York: Macmillan, 1986.

Whitley, Roger, *Assess the IRS!*, New York: Vantage Press, 1978. (A hair-raising story of an endless audit.)